Literature

GRADES 4–6

Enrich your curriculum with teacher-tested ideas based on classic children's literature. *The Best Of* The Mailbox® *Literature* features literature-based teaching units—selected from issues of *The* Intermediate *Mailbox*® magazine, published between 1987 and 1997—that provide an abundance of natural connections to content-area learning. You'll find units that will get your students excited about reading, expand their knowledge and understanding of cultural diversity, provide exemplary models for values education, and offer natural connections to many curricular areas. Inside this invaluable classroom resource, you'll find the following:

- Novel units
- Motivating ideas for getting kids into books
- A bonanza of book report ideas
- Literature-based thematic units
- Thematic booklists
- Hands-on activities

- Independent, small-group, and whole-class activities
- Critical-thinking activities
- Integrated learning
- Skills-based reproducibles

Note to the teacher: *All of the books featured in this fabulous resource were in-print at the time the original magazine units were published. We've taken care to choose featured units and books for this resource that are currently in-print, but we cannot guarantee that every book featured will remain in-print. Should you have trouble locating any of the titles featured herein, check with your media specialist.*

Editor:
Kim T. Griswell

Artists:
Jennifer Tipton Bennett, Cathy Spangler Bruce, Pam Crane, Teresa Davidson, Susan Hodnett, Becky Saunders, Barry Slate, Donna K. Teal

Cover Artist:
Jennifer Tipton Bennett

©1998 by THE EDUCATION CENTER, INC.
All rights reserved.
ISBN #1-56234-251-7

Manufactured in the United States
10 9 8 7 6 5 4 3 2 1

Table Of Contents

Getting Kids Into Books

Motivate your students for a year full of reading fun with the most exciting teacher-tested ideas from the past ten years of the Intermediate edition of The MAILBOX® magazine. Use the ideas on pages 4–10 to entice your students to enter the wonderful world of books.

Keys To Reading Fun

To encourage my students to read at the beginning of the school year, I post a sign labeled "How Can You Help Unlock The Surprise? Read!" I explain that in order to "unlock" the surprise, each student must fill out a construction-paper key for each book that he or she has read. Each key must include the title, author, and main idea of the book. I attach each key to a yarn "key chain." When the key chain reaches a predetermined length, the class is awarded a surprise such as a popcorn party, bookmarks, or a videotape viewing of a previously read book.

Melissa Mathis, St. James of the Valley School, Cincinnati, OH

Awesome Author Displays

To promote literature in my classroom, I create my own author posters. I include pictures of the author (or poet) and short articles that I find in book catalogs, book club newsletters, and *Mailbox* features. I also use the library as a source for information about authors. The posters are decorated with artwork (also found in book catalogs) related to the authors' books, and annotated bibliographies are added. After laminating, I display a poster on a bulletin board or table along with related literature activities and books. These posters are easy to make and are an excellent way to stimulate students' interest in authors and their books.

Darlene Papa, Pasadena, CA

The Bookworm Club

To begin a new school year, I display laminated pictures of bookworms reading books. Each bookworm has a student's name written on it. Every time a student reads a book, he receives a sticker to place on his bookworm. Periodically we have Bookworm Club parties for everyone who's participating. At the end of the year, I take the top three readers out for sundaes. It's a great incentive to get kids to read more books!

Donna Evert—Gr. 4, Phalen Lake Elementary School, St. Paul, MN

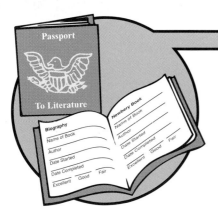

Passport To Literature

I want my students to choose and read a variety of books during the school year. To encourage an assortment of books, I give each student a Passport To Literature booklet at the beginning of the year. The passport consists of a cover and 16 minipages. The minipages include an informational page about the student, three student-choice pages, and 12 pages for recording different types of literature such as historical fiction, modern realistic fiction, biography, poetry, etc. On each minipage, the student writes the title of the book, its author, the dates he began and completed the book, and a rating of the book. To make the passport official, I photograph each student and glue the picture to the inside cover. After completing a book, the student takes his passport to the school media center for an official stamp. By the end of the year, each student has read at least 12 different kinds of books.

Janet Hornbostel—Gr. 5, Richmond School, St. Charles, IL

"Pop"-ular Reading

To encourage our students to read, my school held a "Pop Your Top And Read Day." On that day, students brought cans of pop or juice to school. At a designated time, everyone (including teachers) "popped" open their drink cans and read for 25 minutes. The students enjoyed the novelty of drinking pop in class, and everyone was reminded that reading is fun. The empty cans were donated to our sixth-grade recycling project.

Babette J. Quinn—Gr. 4, Big Thompson Elementary, Loveland, CO

A Definite Ten!

Organize your next book report assignment around the number ten. Have students list ten facts about the book, describe ten characters, detail ten important story events, or list ten reasons why the book was enjoyable. This activity will stretch your students' thinking as they dig deeply into their novels to find the ultimate ten!

Janet Moody—Gr. 4, Truman Elementary, Lafayette, LA

Book Maps

When my class is learning map skills about countries of the world, I have each student read a fiction book. The setting of the book must be in a country other than the United States. As a book-report project, the student creates a map of the country in which the story is set. The capital, main cities, rivers, mountains, and other features are included on the map. It's a great way to combine literature and geography.

Marion Novak—Gr. 5, A. F. Ames School, Riverside, IL

Featured Favorites

I've found a fun way to lure students into our class Reading Corner. At the beginning of the year, each child completes an interest inventory. I use these inventories to help me select books for the Reading Corner. Each week I feature a hobby or recreation and stock the corner with related books. We then sit in a circle as I introduce several of the books. I read aloud from a book; then I stop at a crucial point, close the book, and put it away. Sometimes I just share pictures from a book. I also invite students to suggest interesting books about the featured topic that they've read and to share personal experiences. After our circle time, students rush to the Reading Corner and read, read, read!

Carrie Mayeur, Baton Rouge, LA

Reading Pillowcases

Three times a week my students stop and read for 20 minutes. I noticed that this SSR (Sustained Silent Reading) time did not motivate the majority of students. I decided to increase enthusiasm by having students make SSR pillows. Each student illustrated his favorite book on a 12" x 12" white cotton square. On another cotton square, the student experimented with different ways to write his name. The children then pinned the squares together. Parent volunteers sewed each pillow on 3 1/2 sides. Each child then unpinned his pillow, stuffed it, and hand-sewed the final side together. Now my students love SSR time!

Brenda McGee—Gr. 4, Meadows Elementary School, Plano, TX

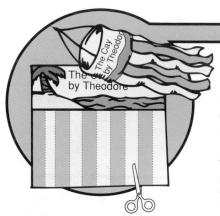

Breezy Book Reports

For a book report of a different sort, try making colorful windsocks. Give each student a 12" x 18" piece of white or light-colored construction paper. Have the child draw a line seven inches from the top edge. In this top section, the student illustrates a scene from his book. Next have the student measure eight to ten strips up to the line as shown. On these strips, the child writes information about his book's characters, plot, setting, ending, etc. He then cuts the strips, rolls the two ends of the windsock together, and tapes securely. Punch holes in the top of each windsock, add yarn, and hang in your classroom for a festive way to motivate even more reading!

Alma Winberry, Great Falls, MT

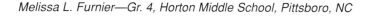

Reading Scavenger Hunt

Send your super sleuths on the trails of reading fun with a scavenger hunt. After reading a novel together, have students complete a scavenger hunt based on the book and its themes. I developed a scavenger hunt on Armstrong Sperry's *Call It Courage*. The story really came alive as my students searched for Polynesian recipes, hunted for the names of Pacific sea animals, and located newspaper articles featuring courageous people. It's a great project to wind up a literature unit.

Melissa L. Furnier—Gr. 4, Horton Middle School, Pittsboro, NC

March Into Reading

To promote their favorite books, students in our school held a schoolwide "Love Of Reading" parade. Each student drew his favorite book cover on a 12" x 18" sheet of construction paper. A head, two arms, and two legs of assorted colors were added. These "marching books" were displayed in all the hallways. A banner entitled "Marching For The Love Of Reading" was hung over the library door. Our students loved this project and talked about their favorite books all month long. Every class, grades K–6, participated. What a big success!

Martha Hart—Librarian, Van Buskirk Elementary School, Tucson, AZ

Newbery Library

Our school media center has a Newbery Club for interested students. To encourage my students to read Newbery and Newbery Honor Books in order to join the club, I keep a collection of these books in a separate "library" within my classroom library. The books are stored in decorated boxes on the top bookshelves of our class library. This Newbery section helps students become more aware of the kinds of books that win this prestigious award each year. Now they don't have to go far to find award-winning books to read!

Barbara Woodward, Albuquerque, NM

Novel Tablecloths

When reading a novel that doesn't have any chapter titles, my students create a novel tablecloth. First I cover a tabletop with white bulletin-board paper. Next I divide the paper into squares (one for each chapter of the book). After reading the first chapter, students divide into small groups and brainstorm possible chapter titles. I list their ideas on a chalkboard; then students vote for their favorite. The winning group writes its title at the top of the first square on the tablecloth, then illustrates a scene that best represents the chapter. It's a lot of fun to see our tabletop art develop as each chapter is read. By the end of the book, we have a colorful tablecloth representing the major events of our book.

Julie Plowman—Gr. 6, Adair-Casey Elementary, Adair, IA

Thumbprint Story Maps

For a fun art project that doubles as a book review, try thumbprint story maps. First have each student draw a squiggly line from one edge of a piece of art paper to the other. Next direct the student to use an ink pad to make thumbprints strategically across this route. As he reads the book, have the student decorate each thumbprint to represent a character or an important item from each chapter read. Your students are sure to give these novel summaries a big thumbs-up!

Debbie Patrick—Gr. 5, Park Forest Elementary, State College, PA

Biography Boxes

After completing a study of biographies, have students create these unique book reports. On a large sheet of tagboard, have each student draw a pattern like the one shown. Have students illustrate the six squares in the pattern with the following: 1) the title and author of the book, a drawing of the biography's person, and the student's name; 2) the person's greatest accomplishment; 3) a sequential list of seven important events in the person's life; 4) any weakness, failure, or disappointment that the person had or experienced; 5) important people in the person's life; and 6) the student's choice of something important about this person. To complete the cube, instruct each student to fold on the dotted lines and tape the sides together. Display these boxed reviews in your media center for others to enjoy.

Julia Alarie—Gr. 6, Essex Middle School, Essex, VT

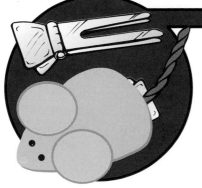

Motivational "Mouse Markers"

These easy-to-make bookmarks motivate students to achieve predetermined reading goals. When a student meets his goal, he is entitled to make a "mouse marker." Hair clips, gray felt, gray yarn, tagboard, glue, scissors, various felt scraps, and instructions are provided at a minicenter. To make a mouse marker, glue together a mouse body cut from tagboard and one cut from gray felt. Attach a yarn tail; then glue the body atop a hair clip. Glue felt ears, eyes, and a nose in place. For variety, cut kite, teddy bear, or seasonal shapes from felt and decorate as markers.

Marilyn Borden, Castleton Elementary School, Bomoseen, VT

Sing Down The Moon

While reading Scott O'Dell's book *Sing Down The Moon,* I have my students write letters to the Departments of Tourism in New Mexico and Arizona. This way we can learn more about the setting of the story by reading the states' brochures and looking at the pictures that are sent. This activity can be done with a variety of books. Your students can read brochures about Denmark and Sweden while reading *Number The Stars,* and information about Oklahoma for *Where The Red Fern Grows.* Check your almanac for current addresses. Your students will enjoy writing for the information and receiving those colorful brochures in the mail.

Ann Nicklawske—Gr. 4, Maternity Of Mary/St. Andrew School, St. Paul, MN

Newbery Contest

At the end of the year—before reading motivation totally wanes—I challenge my students to a Newbery reading contest. If the class reaches a shared goal of reading 100 Newbery books, I treat students to a pizza party. In addition, I reward the top three readers with individual prizes. This contest has my students spending every spare minute reading excellent literature!

Donna Evert—Grs. 4–5, Monroe Elementary, St. Paul, MN

Calling All Readers

Generate enthusiasm about reading by playing "The Home Reading Game." Set aside one or two weeks to play the game. Explain to students that the game is played between 7:00 and 7:15 each evening, Monday through Thursday. The object is for the teacher to catch students in the act of reading. During that time period, the teacher will randomly call the homes of two students each night for the duration of the game. He will ask to speak to an adult who must verify that his or her child is reading or has just finished. (Flexibility is the key, since schedules are tough to maintain.) Those students who get caught reading will be recognized in class the next morning and receive a special treat from the teacher. Students and parents alike enjoy taking part in this activity to encourage reading.

Chris Christensen, Marion B. Earl Elementary, Las Vegas, NV

Movie Making

After reading a popular book together, my class wanted to watch its movie version, as we did earlier in the year with another title. Since there was no movie of this particular book, the class decided to create one! The students planned and wrote a modified script. Then, using the school video camera, we filmed our movie. We all watched it on the last day of school. Everyone was thrilled with our production!

Beth Price—Gr. 5, Logan Intermediate School, Bridgeport, NJ

Scoop Up A Good Book

I encourage my fourth graders to read with a "Get The Scoop!" display. Each student is given a construction-paper ice-cream cone that has five writing lines on the ice cream. Whenever a student completes a book, he writes its title on the first line on the ice cream. When every student in the class has filled his scoop of ice cream with five titles, we celebrate with an ice-cream party! Then we add another ice-cream pattern atop each first one. When everyone's second scoop is filled with book titles, we have another party. We continue this all year long. What a cool reading incentive!

Esther Thompson—Gr. 4, Hendricks, MN

Main-Character Photo Albums

Photographs promise to capture a moment forever—so why not capture the life of a favorite book character by creating a unique photo album? After a book has been read, have each student draw and color at least ten "photographs" that could have belonged to the main character. Have the student cut out each photo, mount it on construction paper (either singly or in groups), and write a caption beneath it. Provide the student with materials for making front and back covers. Have him staple his photo pages inside. Then have him write the title of his book on the front cover and illustrate it. Direct him to write his name on the back cover.

Anna Bordlee—Gr. 5, Boudreaux Elementary, Harvey, LA

Famous Facts

For one of the last book reports of the year, we decided to have our fifth graders read biographies. (Did you know that Biographers Day is celebrated on May 16?) As a culminating activity, we held a Biography Brunch. Each student came to school dressed as his book's character. Time was set aside for each "guest" to share some interesting (and perhaps little-known) facts about him- or herself. Refreshments were supplied by the students. Our kids enjoyed this opportunity to mix with lots of important people from the past and present. As an added bonus, they also learned that biographies can be lots of fun!

Vail Neal and Joyce Garrison—Gr. 5, Presbyterian Day School, Cleveland, MS

New Names

If you're looking for a great book to finish the year, try Virginia Hamilton's novel, *Zeely*. Then follow up the book with a fun activity based on names. Discuss why the children in *Zeely* chose to call themselves Geeder and Toeboy for the summer. Then allow students to choose new names for themselves. Stress to students that each name they choose must have a meaning. To help students, provide a few books that give the meanings and origins of names. Let the students make nameplates for their desks and use their new names for a week!

Diana West, Main Elementary, Rome, GA

Terrific Time Capsules

My sixth graders really enjoy book reports because of a fun project we do. First I give book talks on some of my favorite fantasy and science fiction books. Then students are matched with fantasy and science fiction books of their own to read. The required project is making a time capsule. Each student brings to school a decorated box with five items inside. The items represent themes or objects in the book she read. Each student presents her time capsule to the class and explains the items it contains. What a fun way to present new books!

Lisa Taylor—Gr. 6, Binnsmead Middle School, Portland, OR

What Is This Goop?

Launch your students into an artistic exploration of a book character's personality. Have each student trace a T-shirt shape onto cardboard; then have him cut out the shape. Have the child sketch on scrap paper a design that represents a character in his book. Instruct the student to transfer his design onto the T-shirt shape using a pencil. Meanwhile, mix equal parts of flour, salt, and water. Divide this "goop" among several squirt bottles; then tint each bottle with a different color of tempera paint. Have the students use the goop to outline their designs. After drying overnight, the designs will have a puffed-paint appearance.

Kasi Redfearn—Grs. 4–5, Fredstrom School, Lincoln, NE

Previously Owned Book Sale

To motivate reading during the summer, my class holds a weeklong book sale near the end of the school year. To get ready for the sale, each student is assigned a code letter. With his parent's help, he codes and prices any preschool through sixth-grade books from home that he'd like to sell. After setting up our displays, we invite other classes to the sale. Each of my students receives money for the books he sells, which he can then use to buy "new" books for summer reading. Since they handle all the money, my students learn valuable money skills. They also learn the concept of supply and demand—if a book's price is too high, it may need to be reduced. Not only is our book sale a wonderful learning experience, but it's also a great way to recycle books!

Carolyn Shaw—Gr. 4, Ballard Community Schools, Nevada, IA

Book Report Bonanza

Stop digging in your files for a way to spark your reading program—you've just struck it rich with this treasure trove of book report activities!

Book Report Bonanza

by Linda D. Rourke

BOOK REPORT #1

Type Of Book: Student's choice
Warm-up Activity: Writing a summary
Reproducible Project (page 16): Making a book jacket

Materials Needed:
—markers or crayons
—construction paper

Book Report #1 allows students to read books of their own choosing. The featured skill is writing a summary. Explain to the class that a summary is a condensation of a particular subject. It tells the general idea without going into all the details. When summarizing, it helps to underscore any key words or phrases on the page or in one's mind. Read aloud a chapter from a favorite book. Have students jot down any key words or phrases as you read; then ask each child to write a summary of the chapter. Later, after each student has chosen his book and has read for several days, ask him to write a summary of the last chapter he has read.

When students are well into their books, choose a book and have students examine its cover. Challenge students to list all the important items that are included on the book cover or jacket; then assign the reproducible book jacket project on page 16. Display the books with their new book jackets in the room.

BOOK REPORT #2

Type Of Book: Student's choice
Warm-up Activity: Reading for details
Reproducible (page 17): Making a "PIE-agram"

Materials Needed:
— aluminum pie plate
— brad
— scissors, tape, and glue
— tagboard
— markers or crayons
—index card

Students will read books of their choice for Book Report #2. The skill to work on is reading for details. Explain to the class that they can understand more of what they read if they pay closer attention to the details of the story. Encourage students to become critical readers with a small-group activity. Ask each group to read a newspaper article and note the answers to these questions: *Who* was involved? *What* happened? *When* did it happen? *Where* did it happen? *Why* did it happen? *How* did it happen? Provide time for groups to share their articles and notes.

When students have read half of their books, have each answer the same questions about his story. Assign the reproducible project on page 17. Have students share their completed projects with another class.

A Complete Book Report Program

Book Report Bonanza consists of nine book report activities, enough for an entire year of reading fun. Each book report includes a warm-up activity, a reproducible project, and a special reproducible award. An easy way to manage this program is to assign one book report for each month of the school year. After completing the projects, have students share their work. Not only will students love doing these projects, they'll get hooked on reading for the sheer pleasure of it.

BOOK REPORT #3

Type Of Book: "How-to" book
Warm-up Activity: Sequential order
Reproducible Project (page 18): Giving a demonstration

Materials Needed:
— demonstration supplies

Gather together a selection of how-to books to show your class the variety they have to choose from for Book Report #3. You might try introducing the project by demonstrating an activity that you have learned from a book. Your demonstration can provide the incentive for students to choose an unusual book that will be fun for the entire class. It also will provide the model for a clear, concise demonstration.

The skill to work on is sequential order. Challenge the class to remember the steps involved in your demonstration as you write them on the board. Erase a step and ask students to explain the importance of doing things in the proper order. Assign the reproducible project on page 18. Post a sign-up sheet for student demonstrations (scheduling no more than three in one day).

BOOK REPORT #4

Type Of Book: Student's choice
Warm-up Activity: Using description
Reproducible Project (page 19): Making an advertisement

Materials needed:
— poster board
— crayons or markers

By now, your students will be recommending books that they have enjoyed for Book Report #4. Take time to discuss different books, and spread the word about how fulfilling reading can be.

The skill to be worked on is using description. Make a transparency for a page from a novel. Project the page on the overhead projector and read it aloud. Discuss the use of description. Explain that a good writer uses description to make a story more interesting. Adjectives and adverbs provide added detail and dimension to a story. Demonstrate this point by crossing out all the descriptive words from the story page and reading it again. What conclusions can students draw about the importance of description in writing?

Assign the reproducible project on page 19. Display the posters in the hallway to create a colorful backdrop and encourage reading.

BOOK REPORT #5

Type Of Book: Biography
Warm-up Activity: Taking notes
Reproducible Project (page 20): Role-playing

Materials Needed:
— any necessary props or costumes

    Students will be choosing a biography for Book Report #5. The skill to work on is note taking. Assemble a collection of biographies in the classroom. Include a variety of personalities from such fields as history, sports, science, and entertainment. Read aloud a biographical sketch from a newspaper, magazine, or textbook. Ask students to take notes on the important facts about this person's life.

    As students read their biographies, instruct them to take notes about any interesting events or accomplishments in this person's life. Assign the reproducible project on page 20. Encourage students to come dressed in costume or to set the stage with props, scenery, or music.

BOOK REPORT #6

Materials Needed:
— newsprint or large, unlined manila
  paper
—markers or colored pencils

Type Of Book: Student's choice
Warm-up Activity: Learning the parts of a newspaper
Reproducible Project (page 21): Writing a newspaper

    Book Report #6 allows student to select books of their own choosing. The featured skill is becoming familiar with the different parts of a newspaper. Ask students to bring in copies of newspapers. Divide the class into small groups so that students can examine the papers. Help them to find the following parts: the *masthead* (name of the newspaper), *headline* (title of a news story), *dateline* (tells where the story occurred), *byline* (name of the writer of a news story), *editorial* (article in which editors or citizens express their opinions on a particular subject), *feature* (informational or interest story, not necessarily a top news story), and *classified ads* (used to advertise jobs or items to be bought or sold).

    Students will use their knowledge to create their own newspapers about their books. Assign the reproducible project on page 21. Have students display their newspapers on a bulletin board with the title "Extra! Extra! Read All About It!"

BOOK REPORT #7

Type Of Book: Nonfiction book about a city or country
Warm-up Activity: Making an outline
Reproducible Project (page 22): Making a travel brochure

Materials Needed:
— 8 1/2" x 11" unlined paper
— markers, crayons, or colored pencils

Here's a chance for students to learn about some fascinating places in the world. Each student will be choosing a nonfiction book spotlighting a country or city of his choice. The featured skill is outlining. Tell students that they are going to become as knowledgeable as a travel agent about a particular country or city. Explain that they can organize the information that they read about by putting the facts into an outline. To demonstrate outlining, read an article from a high-interest magazine. Work with your class to make a simple outline of the important facts.

Next assign the reproducible project on page 22. After the travel brochures are completed, stage an event called "Around The World Day." Each student will act as a travel agent, telling about his chosen country or city. Attach a large world map to the wall. Display the brochures around the map. Have students attach pushpins or small flags to the map to identify their featured cities and countries.

BOOK REPORT #8

Type Of Book: Student's choice
Warm-up Activity: Using a glossary
Reproducible Project (page 23): Making a canned book report

Materials Needed:
—large coffee or shortening can
—scissors, crayons or markers, tape, glue, stapler
—lined and unlined paper
—construction paper

Try holding several brief book talks before completing this project. Have students bring to class their favorite books. Hold discussions about story lines, characters, author styles, etc. Your book talks will provide loads of suggestions for this free-choice book report.

The featured skill is using a glossary. Explain to the class that a glossary is a mini-dictionary. It gives the pronunciations and meanings of the more difficult words found in a book. Challenge small groups to choose a textbook and write ten questions that can be answered using the glossary. Have groups switch questions and answer them.

Assign the reproducible project on page 23. Display the canned book reports in the library. They are sure to encourage others to read these spotlighted books.

BOOK REPORT #9

Type Of Book: Nonfiction book on a sport or game
Warm-up Activity: Learning how to teach a skill
Reproducible Project (page 24): Teaching a game

Materials Needed:
—any needed equipment or props

In this final project, each student will read a nonfiction book about a game or sport and teach the class how to play it. Encourage the class to pick unusual or interesting topics. To prepare them for teaching a skill effectively, discuss the important elements that should be included in a lesson. A good lesson states the topic and objective clearly, carries out the objective in a way that holds interest, involves the class in some way, and checks the class's understanding of the topic by actually playing the game. See if students can recall some effective methods you have used in teaching lessons. Brainstorm various techniques that students can employ in their lessons.

Assign the reproducible project on page 24. Post a sign-up sheet for student lessons (scheduling no more than three in one day). Who knows? This could be the start for a future Olympic champion (or weekend duffer) and surely will be the makings of a great deal of classroom excitement.

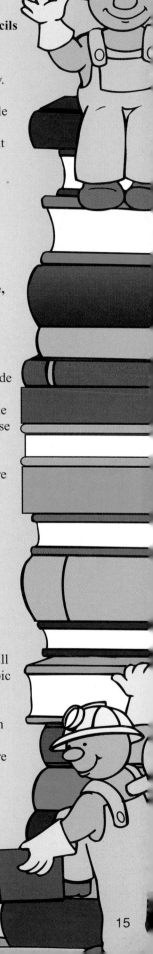

Name _____

Due Date: _____

Back It With A Book Jacket

After you have read your book named _____,
write a summary below. Give a general idea of what the book is about without giving all the
details. _____

_____

_____

_____

_____

_____

Look at the book you have just read. Name six items that are shown on the front, back, and inside covers.

1. _____   4. _____

2. _____   5. _____

3. _____   6. _____

Design a new book jacket by following the directions below. Put a ✓ in the blank as you complete each step.

_____ 1. You will need a piece of construction paper that is larger than your book when the book is
opened. Fold the paper in half lengthwise. Place the center of the book on the center of
the construction paper as shown.

_____ 2. Fold in the top and bottom edges of the paper (A and B) until they are even with the
edges of the book. Crease the folds. Fold under the side edges (C and D) in the same
way, and crease. Slip the cover of the book into the side sleeves to make sure your book
jacket fits; then remove the book.

_____ 3. Design the front cover of the book jacket. Be sure to include the book's
title, author, illustrator, and publisher.

_____ 4. Write a summary of the book on the back cover. Add illustrations.

_____ 5. Add any other information you feel would make the book jacket stand out.

Bonus Box: Add a quote from a "reviewer" who read the book to your book jacket.

16

"Detail-icious" Pie

On an index card, write the title of your book and the answers to these questions:

Time—When did the story take place?	**Characters**—Who were the main characters?
Setting—Where did the story take place?	**Climax**—What was the turning point?
Plot—What happened in the story?	**Conclusion**—How did the story end?

To make a "PIE-agram," add an illustration to each wedge on the detail wheel. Glue it to tagboard and cut it out. Cut out a piece the same size as a wedge from the bottom of an aluminum pie plate. (To protect your fingers, place transparent tape around the edges where you cut the pie plate.) Place the wheel facedown inside the pie plate and attach it with a brad as shown. The wheel should spin freely. On the bottom of the pie plate, add your book's title and author, and your name. Post your index cards with your "PIE-agram."

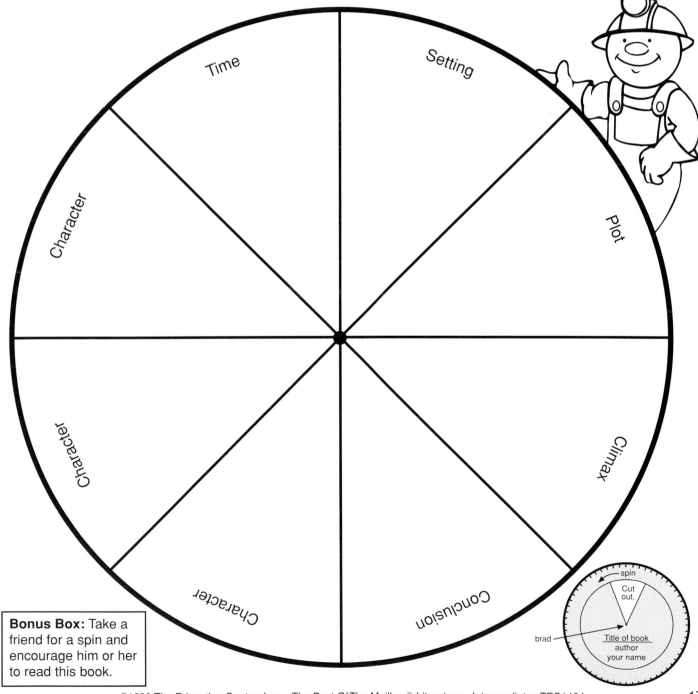

Bonus Box: Take a friend for a spin and encourage him or her to read this book.

It's A Demonstration!

1. Choose a nonfiction, "how-to" book to read. It can be a craft book, cookbook, science experiment book, or hobby book. Since you will be asked to give a demonstration based on the book to the class, be sure the topic really interests you. Your book's title is

_____ .

Today I will show you how to juggle!

2. Read your how-to book. Decide what you will do for your class demonstration. The topic of your demonstration will be _____ .

3. Plan your demonstration. It should last about five minutes. Consider the order of the steps to be presented. List the steps in your demonstration in order below.

_____
_____
_____
_____
_____
_____
_____
_____
_____
_____
_____
_____
_____

4. List all the necessary materials or ingredients for your class demonstration.

_____
_____
_____
_____
_____

5. Practice giving your demonstration at home. Talk clearly. Be sure you understand your topic so you can answer any questions. You are sure to have fun sharing your knowledge with the class!

Bonus Box: Make a sample of your demonstration product to display during your talk.

The ABCs Of Advertising

After you have read your book, _____,
you will be asked to make a poster to advertise it to potential readers. It's as easy as ABC when
you follow these directions:

...stands for **adjectives.** Use adjectives to give details and interest
to your book advertisement without giving away the complete story
line. Consider telling about an interesting event or character.

...stands for **basics.** Include in your advertisement basic information
such as the title of the book, the author's name, your name, and a
short paragraph to entice someone to read this book.

...stands for **color.** The use of color and design is important to draw
attention to your poster. Illustrations are the best eye-catchers.

Plan your poster on a small scale in the box below. Use the above information to help you.

NOW make your advertisement on a large scale using a piece of poster board and crayons or
markers. Post it in a hallway or on a bulletin board for everyone to see.

Name _____

Biography Book Report

In this assignment, you will read a *biography,* which is a factual story about a person's life. This can be a book about an important person in our time or in times past. You can choose to read about a political figure, soldier, inventor, dancer, singer, sports figure, scientist, artist, explorer, entertainer, hero, or any person of interest to you.

1. As you read your biography named _____,
   take notes about the important facts, events, people, time period, or places in the subject's life.

2. Show off your acting ability by stepping into the shoes of this person! You will pretend to be this person in a dramatic presentation to the class. You may dress up and use props, or you can just let class members use their imaginations.

   To prepare this five-minute presentation, you will need to organize your notes and decide which facts will be the most interesting to share. Use the space below to plan and organize your presentation so that you can portray this individual in an interesting way.

   _____
   _____
   _____
   _____
   _____
   _____
   _____
   _____
   _____
   _____
   _____
   _____
   _____
   _____
   _____
   _____

3. Practice your presentation in front of a mirror or with a good friend. Be relaxed. Speak clearly. Have fun with the character!

4. Your presentation date is _____.

Newspaper Book Report

The Daily News

1. You'll be using the information from your book, _____ _____, to make a newspaper. Begin by reading all of the boxes on this page.

The Daily News

2. Now that you've read the boxes, you're ready to **plan** your newspaper. It should have a *front page* plus three other pages for a total of four pages.

The Daily News

3. After you've planned your newspaper, you're ready to make a **rough draft.** Check off each of the boxes 5–11 as you complete the activities. Don't forget to leave room for illustrations.

The Daily News

4. **Proofread your rough draft** carefully and make any changes. Now you're ready to make a **final copy.** Use newsprint or paper with a newspaper look. Print or type the words clearly; then add your illustrations.

The Daily News

5. ____ Choose a *name* for your newspaper. Be sure the name has something to do with your book. Include a *date, publisher's name,* and *price* for your newspaper. Put this information on the front page.

The Daily News

6. ____ On the front page, write at least two *news stories* about events from the book. Think of catchy *headlines* for the stories. Include illustrations.

The Daily News

7. ____ Write an *editorial section* that includes:
   - an editorial giving your opinion about a character or event in the book
   - a letter to the editor giving another opinion about a character or event in the book

The Daily News

8. ____ Write a *feature section* that includes:
   - an article of interest about one of your book's characters, places, or social activities
   - background information about any subject mentioned in the book

The Daily News

9. ____ Write an *entertainment section* that includes any of the following:
   - a comic strip
   - a word search or crossword puzzle
   - a joke for the day
   Each item in this section must use a book character or event.

The Daily News

10. ____ Write a *classified ads section* that includes:
   - two ads for items mentioned in the book that could be sold or wanted by others
   - two ads for jobs similar to jobs mentioned in the book

The Daily News

11. ____ Suggestions for other sections include:
   - *an advice column*
   - *a sports page*
   - *a stock market report*
   - *TV or movie listing*
   - *store advertisements*

The Daily News

12. Remember the steps for making a good newspaper:
   1. **Planning**
   2. **Writing a rough draft**
   3. **Proofreading and making changes**
   4. **Writing the final copy**
   Due date: _____

Be A Travel Agent

In this assignment, you'll read a nonfiction book about a city or country. You'll then design a travel brochure about your chosen place. Read your book, _____, and take notes. Then organize your notes into the following outline. Fill in the outline for the first main topic—location. Next choose four more main topics from this list and write them in the outline: climate, sites of interest, food, clothing, topography, language, history, government, recreation. Complete the outline using your notes.

Place: _____

I. **Location**
   A. _____
   B. _____
   C. _____

II. _____
   A. _____
   B. _____
   C. _____

III. _____
   A. _____
   B. _____
   C. _____

IV. _____
   A. _____
   B. _____
   C. _____

V. _____
   A. _____
   B. _____
   C. _____

To complete your travel brochure, follow these directions:
1. Fold an 8 1/2" x 11" piece of white paper into thirds.
2. On the first third, add the place, an illustration of it, and your name.
3. On each of the five remaining sections, include information that you learned about the five main topics above. Include any illustrations, maps, or notes of interest.

Due Date: _____

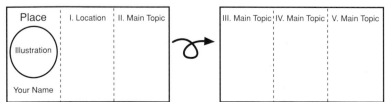

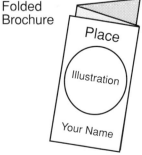

Folded Brochure

Bonus Box: Be a travel agent for a day. Give an exciting talk to your class about your city or country.

Name _____ Making a canned book report, writing a glossary

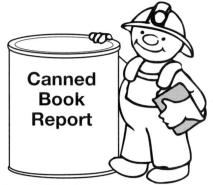

After reading your book _____,
you will make a complete, "can-sized" review of it. Just follow the
directions below. Check off (✓) each activity as you complete it.

Canned Book Report

_____ 1. You'll need a large coffee or shortening can with a reusable, plastic lid. Cut a piece of
construction paper to fit around the can. Using crayons or markers, draw an eye-catching
scene from your book on the paper. Tape or glue the scene around the outside of the can.

_____ 2. Make a glossary of the difficult words from your book. Make it in the form of a booklet.
Choose a size to fit into your can. Use lined paper for the glossary. For each word, include the pronunciation, definition, and a sentence showing how to use that word. Staple
a construction-paper cover to your glossary.

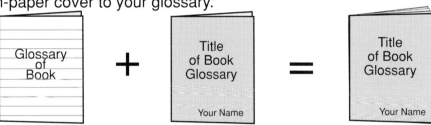

_____ 3. Make another booklet giving a summary of the book. Tell just enough to create interest
without giving away the story line.

_____ 4. Make a filmstrip of your favorite part of the book. Follow the directions below.

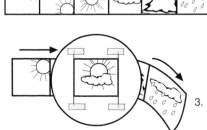

1. Cut a strip of
paper 2" x 10".
Divide into
frames and
illustrate
filmstrip.

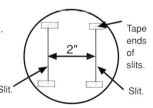

2. Make 2 slits in can lid about 2 1/2"
long and 2" apart.

3. Thread filmstrip
through slits in lid.

4. Tape filmstrip ends to make
a loop.

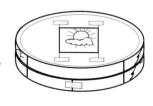

_____ 5. Put all the ingredients into the can and share it with a friend.

Due Date: _____

Bonus Box: Make puppets of the main characters. Choose a size to fit into the can. Create your puppets using
paper, fabric, Popsicle® sticks, pipe cleaners, empty toilet-paper tubes, socks, yarn, clay, etc. Label each puppet.

Name _____

Sports And Games Book Report

After you have read your nonfiction book on sports and games, choose one interesting game or sport to present to your classmates. Your goal will be to teach the class how to play this game or sport. To help you to get ready for your class lesson, fill in the information about your game below. Be sure to use any necessary visual aids like sports equipment, diagrams on a chalkboard or poster, or demonstrations.

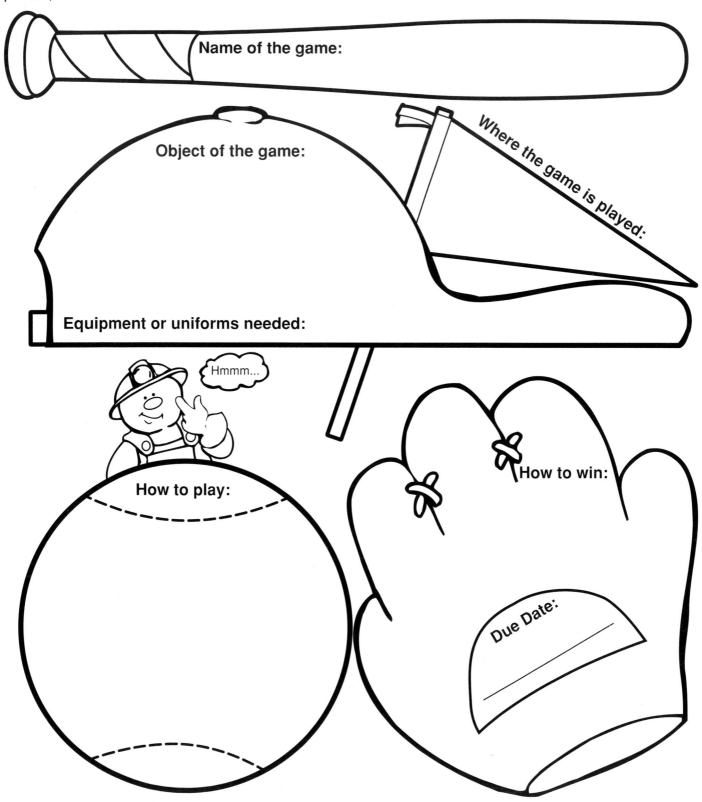

Name of the game:

Object of the game:

Where the game is played:

Equipment or uniforms needed:

Hmmm...

How to play:

How to win:

Due Date: _____

Book Report Bonanza Awards

Duplicate and cut apart. Distribute to students as they finish each book report project.

Book Jacket Project

student

Here's A Pocketful Of Praise For Your Book Jacket!

©1998 The Education Center, Inc.

Demonstration Project

What A Demonstration!

student

©1998 The Education Center, Inc.

"PIE-agram" Project

Given to: _____

Silver Spoon Award

©1998 The Education Center, Inc.

Poster Project

You Really Sold Me! Great Poster!

student

©1998 The Education Center, Inc.

Book Report Bonanza Awards

Duplicate and cut apart. Distribute to students as they finish each book report project.

Biography Project

Actor's Award

for excellence
in
character portrayal

Given to:

_____
student

Travel Brochure Project

_____
student

Travel Agent of the Year

❖ ✳ ❖ ✳ ❖ ✳ ❖

Newspaper Project

Pulitzer Prize
for wonderful writing in your
Newspaper Book Report!

Awarded to: _____

Canned Book Report Project

To: _____

Freshest Homegrown
Canned
Book Report

Sports And Games Project

GOLD MEDAL AWARD

_____
student

Thematic Literature Units

You'll find topics to enrich your curriculum throughout the year in this fabulous collection of thematic literature units from your friends at The MAILBOX® magazine.

All Aboard The Good Ship Friendship

Literature And Teaching Suggestions On The Theme Of Friendship

*There are gold ships,
There are silver ships,
But there's no ship
Like friendship.*

Chart your course toward a positive and productive school year by hoisting up the mainsail of friendship in your classroom. The following books and activities will help you to navigate your class through the fundamentals of friendship.

by Christine A. Thuman

Novels

The Animal, The Vegetable, & John D Jones

Written by Betsy Byars & Illustrated by Ruth Sanderson
Published by Delacorte Press

Clara and Deanie constantly compete for the attention of their divorced father. However, both are dismayed when they learn that they will have to share their vacation with their father's friend Delores and her obnoxious son John D. Tensions rise as the children look for ways to make each other miserable. Then Clara makes a dreadful mistake, and everyone learns how tragedy and loss can transform attitudes.

Students can relate to personality conflict such as that shared between John D and the girls in this story. When people deliberately set out to make life miserable for others, they often succeed. On the flip side, deliberate acts of kindness can create an atmosphere of trust and friendship. Start your year affirmatively by collaborating on an Amicable Acts calendar. Make or purchase a blank poster-sized calendar. Label it "Amicable Acts for [name of month]." Lead students to brainstorm 25 or more benevolent behaviors that would promote a friendly atmosphere in the classroom (encourage someone who seems unhappy, help someone without him knowing it was you, etc.). Transfer the edited ideas onto cards cut to fit inside the calendar squares. Each morning select a student to draw one of the cards and to post it on the calendar. Challenge the students to practice the Amicable Act for the day. Leave a sheet of tiny stickers near the calendar. Whenever a student is a recipient of an Amicable Act, allow the child to place a sticker on that card.

Stay Away From Simon!

Written by Carol Carrick & Illustrated by Donald Carrick
Published by Clarion Books

Lucy and her younger brother Josiah examine their feelings about a mentally handicapped boy they both fear when he follows them home one snowy day. Set in Martha's Vineyard in the 1830's, this story honestly examines some of the fears and misunderstandings that still surround the handicapped.

If Simon lived today, he would probably attend school and receive special help instead of being ostracized. Use this story as a springboard for discussing some of the uncomfortable feelings that can surface when students encounter handicapped individuals. Ask the students: "Why did Simon follow Lucy? What did he really want from her? What caused Lucy to misunderstand Simon's behavior?" As an additional challenge, adopt a special education class in your school. After inviting the special education teacher to come in and discuss the special needs, differences, and similarities of the adoptees, pair or group students from each class together. Call yourselves The Goodwill Ambassador Club and schedule times when club members from each class can get together for peer tutoring, sharing, or playing. Gather your class together after each meeting to reflect on what they've learned about themselves and others.

Hello, My Name Is Scrambled Eggs
Written by Jamie Gilson & Illustrated by John Wallner
Published by Lothrop, Lee & Shepard Books

Harvey Trumble embarks on a heroic mission to mold Vietnamese newcomer Tuan Nguyen into an American. With humor and insight, the author explores the challenge of adjusting to a new culture.

Harvey's willingness to understand a different world culture helped him to befriend Tuan. Begin your class's journey into cultural understanding by defining culture as "the customary beliefs, social forms, and material traits of a particular group of people." Next compare and contrast the American and Vietnamese cultures as revealed in the novel. Finally have each of your students pack a "Society Suitcase." After selecting and reading a nonfiction book about a people from another culture, tell each student to choose six to eight objects that represent that culture and pack them into a small suitcase. (If a student doesn't have access to a suitcase, he can use a brown paper grocery bag and call it a "Society Sack.") Instruct the student to enclose a description of each item and why it is important in that society. Tell students to be prepared to share their Society Suitcase information with the rest of the class. Students can decorate their suitcases with student-made travel stickers, flags, or even travel photos of their cultures.

The Fastest Friend In The West
Written by Vicki Grove
Published by G. P. Putnam's Sons

When Lori's best friend dumps her to hang out with the popular girls, overweight Lori shares an unusual but brief friendship with a homeless girl. With compassion and honesty, this story reveals the troubled lives of two lonely girls, one longing for acceptance and the other for a home.

Intermediate students will identify with the awkwardness of peer relations and the desire for popularity featured in Vicki Grove's book. This story presents the events from both characters' points of view, giving the reader insight into the true feelings behind the characters' actions. As you discuss the story, ask, "How do the characters in this story behave in order to cover up their true feelings? How are these actions misinterpreted?" Invite students to share experiences when their feelings were hurt because of a misunderstanding. After the discussion, provide groups of students with the following scenarios to role-play:
- Ray asks Brian to play tag during recess. Brian declines the invitation. Ray doesn't talk to Brian for the rest of the day.
- Chelsey and Shyreeta have been sitting together during lunch for weeks. One day Chelsey walks into the lunchroom to find Shyreeta sitting with the new girl who just moved into town.
- Chris and Robert spend break looking at Chris's baseball card collection. Chris makes fun of Robert's new haircut. Later Chris notices that one of his cards is missing.

Allow the students to take turns role-playing the events. Try giving the same event to different groups to see some different interpretations.

The Friendship
Written by Mildred D. Taylor & Illustrated by Max Ginsburg
Published by Dial Books For Young Readers

Four children witness a confrontation between an elderly black man and a white storekeeper in rural Mississippi in the 1930s. This story examines the limits that prejudice and misunderstanding can place on a friendship.

This story will surely elicit some strong reactions about what it means to be a good friend. Have the students do some reflective writing, focusing on the tragedy and the attitudes and events that led up to it. Could it have been prevented? What would have happened if Old Tom had not gone into the store for the second time? What might have happened to John if he had kept his vow of friendship and stood up for Old Tom? Were these men ever true friends? Lead the students to put their thoughts into pictures by having them draw a "Diagram Of A True Friend." First brainstorm a list of things that true friends do for one another. Then work together to state these ideas so that they become appropriate captions for a diagram of a human body (always willing to lend a helping **hand**, there when you need a **shoulder** to cry on, **"nose"** when to stay out of your business, etc.). Give each group of three or four children a large sheet of bulletin-board paper. Have them select one student to lie down on the paper, arms and legs extended slightly. Let the other students use a marker to trace the outline of the reclining student. Then encourage the members to fill in details and label the parts to complete a "Diagram Of A True Friend."

Picture Books

Rosie And Michael

Written by Judith Viorst
Illustrated by Lorna Tomei
Published by Atheneum

What makes a friend a friend? In this delightfully illustrated book, two friends unabashedly reveal the makings of their friendship.

How lucky we are when we find that special friend who understands us and can live with our quirks! Help students examine the limitations of friendship by exploring the relationship of Rosie and Michael. Draw two columns on the chalkboard. Label one "Rosie" and the other "Michael." Under the Rosie column, list verb phrases that describe things that Rosie does to show she's a good friend (says I look good, remembers my nicknames, takes a joke, etc.). Repeat this process under the Michael column. Compare and discuss the two columns in light of the saying, "The best way to have a friend is to be a friend." Then have each student label two columns on her own paper: "Things I Look For In A Friend" and "Things That Make Me A Good Friend." As students list their own verb phrases, challenge them to elaborate by giving specific examples from their own experiences of friendship. Finally have each student select ideas from her columns to rewrite into an essay entitled "Why We Should Be Friends." As a final product, bind these essays into a *Good Buddy Booklet*.

The Doorbell Rang

Written & Illustrated by Pat Hutchins
Published by Greenwillow Books

Each time the doorbell rings, someone else comes in to share Ma's wonderful cookies. This delightful tale illustrates how sharing and caring can multiply love and friendship.

Just how far can a person go when it comes to sharing Ma's delicious chocolate chip cookies? Your students will enjoy speculating what might have happened if Grandma had not shown up with more cookies. After the discussion, use your math skills to figure out why the cookies came out evenly distributed each time a new batch of children came over. Take your students deeper by asking them how the multiples of a number are similar to the elements of a friendship. What are some elements of friendship that, when properly multiplied, will produce lasting friends? After students have brainstormed a list of friendship elements or ingredients, let each child draw a large, round chocolate chip cookie onto brown construction paper. On these cookies, have the students list their favorite friendship elements under the title "This Friendship Cookie Contains The Following Minimum Daily Requirements." Have them complete their lists by discussing how much of each element would be necessary to make a wholesome friendship. Then let students add the measurement amounts (2 g, 35 mg etc.). Post the cookies on a bulletin board with the title "Don't Let These Cookies Crumble!"

Wilfrid Gordon McDonald Partridge

Written by Mem Fox & Illustrated by Julie Vivas
Published by Kane/Miller Book Publishers

A small boy sets out to discover the meaning of memory *so that he can help an elderly friend, Miss Nancy, find hers.*

Bring in a basket of eclectic items such as an old watch, a baby bootie, an antique flatiron, a pair of spectacles, a toy car, etc. Give each child one item from the basket. Have the child free-write about that item, recording any thoughts or memories that item brings to mind. Briefly allow willing students to share. Note how many of those memories come from friendship relationships. Using *friendship* as an abstract term, brainstorm definitions of friendship, giving specific examples from life situations. (For example, "Friendship is Kathy giving me her goldfish after she found out that mine died.") Combine the favorite definitions into a class collaborative poem entitled "Friendship Is…."

Best Friends
Written & Illustrated by Steven Kellogg
Published by Dial Books For Young Readers

Kathy and Louise are best friends. They share everything from chocolate milk to their make-believe horse, Silverwind. But then Louise gets carted off to spend two weeks of the summer with her aunt and uncle. How will Kathy deal with her feelings of loneliness?

Even the best of friends can feel jealousy, anger, and loneliness. Ask students if they've ever lost a best friend and how it made them feel. What are the pros and cons of having one best friend? Name some things a person could do to cope with the temporary or permanent loss of a friend. Next provide students with a variety of photographs of masks, as well as a collection of construction paper and scraps of colorful decorative papers. Instruct each student to construct a life-size mask depicting an emotion that he has felt during a friendship. Have each student write a brief explanation of the event on an index card. Post the completed masks and cards on a bulletin board labeled "The Many Faces Of Friendship."

Clancy's Coat
Written by Eve Bunting
Illustrated by Lorinda Bryan Cauley
Published by Viking Kestrel

Even the best of friends sometimes offend one another. In this heartwarming tale, two estranged friends reunite over an old coat that, like their friendship, needs some mending.

I Like You, If You Like Me: Poems Of Friendship
Selected & Edited by Myra Cohn Livingston
Published by Margaret K. McElderry Books

From the tentative exploration of new and blossoming friendships to the painful moments of fighting and reconciling, the many aspects of friendship are explored in this anthology.

Ask your students to share instances when they have inadvertently offended someone with a careless word or deed. In *Clancy's Coat,* Clancy takes a first tentative step toward reconciliation by asking Tippett to repair his coat. What steps have your students taken to mend damaged relationships? Split your class into six to eight groups, and assign each group a different poem from chapter 8 of *I Like You, If You Like Me.* After reading its poem, have each group discuss and record its reflections. Use the following questions and statement to stimulate discussion: "What does this poem reveal about the down side of friendship?" Have you ever acted like the person described in the poem? Tell about a time when you felt like the person in the poem." Finally have each group share its poem and the collaborative reflections with the entire class.

A Collage Of Cultures

Multicultural Books And Suggestions For Their Use

Just watch the nightly news and you'll see signs of a disturbing reality. Incidences of cultural misunderstanding are on the rise. Different racial, ethnic, and cultural groups battle each other, failing to accept and appreciate the diversity that is America today. And even though educators have known for years that children achieve greater success and higher self-esteem when they see themselves and their community reflected in the curriculum, too many students still must strain to find themselves in the textbooks before them.

Yet there is hope, and it's found right in our classrooms and libraries. Teachers are flocking to the library shelves to find excellent books that reflect the multiculturalism of our world. Since one of the goals of *The MAILBOX®* magazine is to help make your job easier, we asked children's book reviewer Deborah Zink Roffino to suggest excellent multicultural picture books and novels for intermediate students. On the following pages, you'll find her recommendations, along with teaching suggestions to extend reading. And for a complete teaching unit on a multicultural title, see pages 92–96 featuring Laurence Yep's wonderful novel *Dragonwings*.

by Becky Andrews and Christine A. Thuman

Drylongso
Written by Virginia Hamilton & Illustrated by Jerry Pinkney
Published by Harcourt Brace Jovanovich, Publishers

In this haunting, lengthy picture book with subtle environmental overtones, a black family coping with the dusty ravages of drought is aided by a mysterious boy named Drylongso. While the family huddles inside their house during a dust storm, Drylongso complains that "if folks would stop plowing where they shouldn't, the dust would settle down."

Use Hamilton's fine tale to introduce a miniunit on soil conservation. Divide students into groups; then provide each group with encyclopedias and resource books on soil conservation. In front of the students, open a large manila envelope that has been addressed to the class. Pull out a letter and several leaves, twigs, and other pieces of greenery. Tell the groups that the letter is from Mother Earth, who has just hired them to stop the soil erosion that is causing dust storms all over the world. Have each group research ways to prevent soil erosion and prepare a presentation outlining its solutions to the problem.

The Greatest Of All: A Japanese Folktale
Retold by Eric A. Kimmel
Illustrated by Giora Carmi
Published by Holiday House, Inc.

Lovely Chuko has chosen Ko Nezumi, the humble field mouse, to be her husband. But Father Mouse doubts the worthiness of this choice. He takes a long and circular trek to find Chuko the greatest of all husbands.

The haiku poem at the end of this story sums up its lessons of modesty and patience. Explain the pattern of haiku poetry to students. Each poem has three lines with five syllables in the first line, seven in the second line, and five in the third line. Read aloud haiku from books such as *Flower • Moon • Snow: A Book Of Haiku* by Kazue Mizumura. Challenge students to write their own haiku poetry. Have them copy their edited poems onto white or gray paper that has been cut in the shape of small boulders. Post these cutouts on a bulletin board, constructing a wall like the one in the story. Add the caption "Tunneling Through With Haiku" and a cut-out mouse peeking out from between two of the stones.

The Woman Who Outshone The Sun: The Legend Of Lucia Zenteno
Written by Alejandro Cruz Martinez & Illustrated by Fernando Olivera
Published by Children's Book Press

Based on a Zapotec legend from Mexico, this luminous picture book tells the story of Lucia, a quiet beauty so re-markable that some people said she outshone the sun. Though instantly beloved by the older people of her village, Lucia is rejected by younger neighbors and leaves the village. Unfortunately for the villagers, Lucia takes with her the river and all things natural that love her.

Use this poetic tale to introduce students to a fun-filled day focusing on folktales from Central and Latin America. Ask your librarian to help you locate four or five other books featuring Hispanic folktales and legends (see the suggestions below). Give a book to each group to read. Then have groups spend the day completing various book-related projects such as reenacting the story, making bumper stickers to advertise the moral of the legend, rewriting the legend as a news-paper article, and designing a new book cover for the tale. At day's end, have students compare and contrast the various legends and choose their favorite.

Suggested books to use:
Borreguita And The Coyote: A Tale From Ayutla Mexico
by Verna Aardema
The Rooster Who Went To His Uncle's Wedding:
A Latin American Folktale by Alma Flor Ada
And Sunday Makes Seven by Robert Baden
Rosa & Marco And The Three Wishes
by Barbara Brenner
Moon Rope by Lois Ehlert

Onion Tears
Written by Diana Kidd
Illustrated by Lucy Montgomery
Published by Orchard Books

In this poignant short novel, Nam-Huong must adjust to her new life in America without the family she left behind in war-torn Vietnam. Though taunted and isolated by her classmates, Nam cries only when chopping onions in Auntie's restaurant. With the help of a sensitive teacher, the lonely refugee is gradually freed from the harrowing memories that haunt her.

It took the kindness of Miss Lily to unlock Nam's heart and unleash the grief that bound it. After reading this short novel to the class, discuss the acts of kindness that began to coax Nam out of her shell. Let students tell about acts of kindness in their own experi-ences that have made a difference in someone's life. Keep the discussion alive for days by challenging stu-dents to comb through newspapers and newsmagazines for articles and pictures about people being kind to others. Provide time each morning for several stu-dents to share their clippings; then post the items on a bulletin board entitled "Kindness Always Makes A Difference."

Mountains To Climb
Written by Richard M. Wainwright & Illustrated by Jack Crompton
Published by Family Life Publishing

"In every person's life there will be many mountains to climb… some harder than others but most conquerable…*one step at a time.*" With these words ringing in his ears and heart, Roberto and his pet llama leave their beloved Andes Mountains to live in America with his aunt and uncle. Facing a new country and a new culture is Roberto's mountain to climb.

Believing that people should not be judged by appearances or dis-abilities, Roberto challenges his new American friends to focus on similarities rather than differences. After sharing this book, divide the class into partners. Form two large circles—one inside the other—with partners facing each other. Have the students list categories of ques-tions (home, hobbies, dislikes, favorites, talents, family, opin-ions about current events, etc.) to ask their partners in or-der to get to know them better. Tell students that they will have 30 seconds to find out five things they have in common with their partners. Encourage creative ques-tioning so that students don't rely on physical similari-ties such as skin color or sex. Set a kitchen timer; then have students interview each other, jotting down similarities on their papers. At the end of the time period, have students in the inner circle move to their right so they are facing new part-ners. Start the timer again and continue as time al-lows. At the end of the activity, let students share surprising insights they gained about their classmates.

Native American Animal Stories

Written by Joseph Bruchac
Illustrated by John Kahionhes Fadden and David Kanietakeron Fadden
Published by Fulcrum Publishing

In this rich collection, 24 tales display the importance of animals in Native American traditions. The finely detailed pen-and-ink sketchings by Mohawk artists John Kahionhes Fadden and David Kanietakeron Fadden take readers back to a time when the earth was young and "man and the animals could speak to each other." After sharing several of the brief tales (perfect for filling up an extra five minutes during the day), explain to students that some Native Americans made memory scrolls to help them recall stories and songs. Assign a story to each pair of students. Give each pair a large grocery bag to cut open and decorate with symbols or pictures to help recall the tale. After decorating the bag, have students crumple it up and then smooth it out to soften the paper. Have each pair display its memory scroll and use it to retell the story orally to their classmates or other classes.

Fiesta!: Mexico's Great Celebrations

Written by Elizabeth Silverthorne
Illustrated by Jan Davey Ellis
Published by The Millbrook Press

Like the confusion of confetti tumbling from a bright piñata, this colorful book is an explosion of information about the fiestas of Mexico. Religious, patriotic, and historical celebrations are described in fascinating detail, including simple recipes and art projects.

In addition to fiestas, murals are commonplace on buildings in Mexico as well as in southern California and U.S. cities elsewhere with large Mexican-American populations. Combine Mexico's love of fiestas and mural painting with a cooperative group activity. Divide a large sheet of butcher paper into several equal-sized panels (one per group); then assign students to several cooperative groups. Assign an important Mexican fiesta to each group. After a group has reread the section describing its festival, have the students complete a rough draft of a mural panel illustrating its fiesta. Students should incorporate helpful captions, including pronunciations and definitions of Spanish terms whenever possible. (The author has included a convenient glossary in the back of her book.) Let the groups work one at a time on the mural. On the day the mural is completed, hold your own minifiesta complete with Mexican hot chocolate and sugar cookies called *polvorones*. You'll find recipes for both in this illuminating book!

Chancay And The Secret Of Fire: A Peruvian Folktale

Written & Illustrated by Donald Charles
Published by G. P. Putnam's Sons

Inspired by an ancient Peruvian tapestry, this bright folktale is the story of Chancay, a humble fisherman who pulls a remarkable fish from the sea. After a series of trials, the fish grants Chancay's wish to bring fire to his people. After sharing this book, discuss the folktale's explanations for such natural phenomena as fire, stars, and the movements of the Sun and Moon. Challenge groups of students to write and illustrate short Chancay tales to answer the following questions about natural phenomena:

• Why is there day and night?
• Why is the Earth round?
• Why is the tiger striped?
• Why do tides go in and out?
• How were thunder and lightning created?
• What causes volcanoes?
• Why is the ocean salty?
• Why don't fish have legs?

Yang The Youngest And His Terrible Ear
Written by Lensey Namioka & Illustrated by Kees De Kiefte
Published by Houghton Mifflin

The Yangs have recently relocated to Seattle from China. Yingtao, the youngest of four children, has a terrible musical ear. How can he tell his musically talented parents that he would rather play baseball than the violin? This lighthearted tale illuminates Chinese culture and treats the reader to an immigrant's perspective on all things American.

Before reading the story aloud, have each student make a listening grid like the one shown. Instruct each child to jot notes in the appropriate columns as she listens. As a fun follow-up to the novel, have your students create watercolor panel paintings. Observe and discuss the Chinese style of painting using pictures from art books. (One excellent selection is *A Young Painter: The Life And Paintings Of Wang Yani—China's Extraordinary Young Artist* by Zheng Zhensun and Alice Low.) For each pair of students, cut a 1' x 3' panel from white bulletin-board paper. Instruct each pair to design and paint a local countryside scene. Have each child sign her work with a signature *chop*—a stamp of the child's initials—made from foam insulation tape mounted on small blocks of wood or heavy cardboard.

The Ancient Cliff Dwellers Of Mesa Verde
Written by Caroline Arnold & Photographed by Richard Hewett
Published by Clarion Books

Packed with fascinating photographs of what is now Mesa Verde National Park in Colorado, this informative book draws the reader into the world of the Anazasi, an ancient people who settled on and suddenly vanished from this famous plateau. Use Arnold's book as a key to unlock the mysteries of this Native American society. Before reading the book, divide your class into four cooperative research groups: anthropologists, archaeologists, botanists, and zoologists. Define these scientific fields and brainstorm the kinds of information that each field would cover. Read the book aloud, instructing each group to record pertinent information. Provide additional resource materials, and instruct the groups to prepare reports. Have groups include student-made artifacts, dioramas, role-playing skits, and models to visually enhance their data. When groups have finished their reports, gather the class into a circle, seating group members together. With the teacher as moderator, hold a seminar-type discussion, drawing upon student research to piece together the cultural puzzle of the Anazasi.

The Road To Memphis
Written by Mildred D. Taylor
Published by Dial Books For Young Readers

During her last year of high school in Mississippi, Cassie Logan faces the harsh realities of southern life in 1941. While America is calling her sons to defend her against foreign adversaries, there lies an enemy within—a deeply rooted bigotry toward blacks—which threatens Cassie's family and friends far more than any distant war.

Read this book to your more mature students and be prepared for challenging discussions on human rights and responsibilities. Create a positive framework for reflection by using the seven principles of Kwanzaa, an African-American holiday based on African harvest festivals and celebrated yearly in December. These principles—unity, self-determination, collective work, cooperative economics, purpose, creativity, and faith—are demonstrated by many of the characters in *The Road To Memphis*. Make a small blank booklet for each Kwanzaa principle; then choose seven students to be recorders and give each recorder a booklet. As you read, ask the class to give examples of Kwanzaa principles as practiced by the characters. Have the appropriate recorder paraphrase each example in his booklet. Place these booklets in your reading center through December to honor Kwanzaa.

Number The Stars
Written by Lois Lowry
Published by Houghton Mifflin Company

During the Nazi reign of terror in Denmark, young Annemarie Johansen must learn the meaning of bravery. Her heart-stopping story highlights the valor of Danish families who risked their lives to smuggle Jews out of Denmark to freedom in Sweden. Your students will enjoy dramatizing the suspenseful episodes from this story.

Begin with a warm-up activity. Select a feeling—anger, joy, surprise, fear, boredom, etc.—and encourage students to close their eyes and recall a time when they felt that emotion. Have them open their eyes and make facial expressions for that feeling. Then instruct students to express the feeling vocally. Finally have them stand and act out the feeling using their entire bodies.

Next list various episodes from the story—the girls running into Nazi soldiers on the street, the soldiers barging into the Johansen home at four o'clock in the morning, Annemarie encountering the soldiers and dogs on the footpath, etc.—on separate index cards. Divide your class into groups. Hand each group a card and instruct the members to act out its episode. Let groups take turns performing their skits for the entire class. Stretch students' acting abilities further by having them reenact the skits through pantomime.

The Girl Who Loved Caterpillars
Adapted by Jean Merrill & Illustrated by Floyd Cooper
Published by Philomel Books

Free-spirited Izumi would rather collect caterpillars and spend time with scruffy peasant boys than concern herself with attracting the right husband. Her story, translated from a 12th-century Japanese scroll, continues to speak to nonconformists everywhere.

Share Izumi's love of nature by taking your class on a nature walk. Provide each pair of students with a specimen carrier such as a lidded jar with air holes punched in the lid. Instruct pairs to carefully collect a variety of bug specimens. Identify the creatures using field guides. Have each student report on the physical characteristics and habitat of one bug. Let each child create a collage of his creature, modeling it after Eric Carle's brilliant illustrations in *The Very Hungry Caterpillar* and *The Very Quiet Cricket.* Instruct each student to cut shapes from colorful fabric and arrange them on a large sheet of white construction paper to form his bug's body. Have the student glue the scraps in place and add details with markers. Display these eye-catching creations with the bug reports on a bulletin board entitled "The Class That Loved Bugs."

The Jade Stone: A Chinese Folktale
Adapted by Caryn Yacowitz
Illustrated by Ju-Hong Chen
Published by Holiday House, Inc.

In this Chinese folktale, Chan Lo, a master carver, is hired by the Emperor to cut a fiery dragon from a flawless hunk of shimmering jade. Listening carefully to the jade before he cuts, Chan Lo hears soft sounds emanating from the stone, a timbre that tells his heart that this piece is not destined to be a dragon. Will he defy the command of the great Emperor?

After sharing this lovely picture book with your students, discuss how Chan Lo—at great risk—stayed true to himself. Ask, "Have you ever had to stand up for yourself even though doing so was risky? How did you feel? What were the results of your stand? Would you do it again? Why or why not?"

After the discussion, have a little fun stretching students' imaginations. Instruct students to close their eyes and imagine that they are each a huge, glimmering piece of dark green jade (which is very prized in China). As students are imagining, ask them to think about what animal they would want to be carved into. Have students open their eyes and free-write about their animal and reasons for their choices. Let volunteers share their ideas with the class.

My Grandmother's Stories: A Collection Of Jewish Folk Tales
Written by Adèle Geras & Illustrated by Jael Jordan
Published by Alfred A. Knopf, Inc.

In ten short stories, the author presents the memories of a young Jewish girl living in Europe before World War II. Each time the young girl plays with a family possession—the button box, Aunt Sara's shoes, Grandmother's shawls—her grandmother shares a family story accompanied by a folktale. These enlightening tales reveal much about traditional Jewish customs while teaching the universal virtues of patience, honesty, and generosity.

Many of the young girl's memories depend heavily on her sense of smell. Find out how well your students distinguish smells by conducting the following experiment: Collect five to ten samples of the heavily scented items mentioned in Gera's stories, such as nutmeg, cinnamon, cheese, herring, pine needles, roses, onions, chopped liver, soap, aniseed (licorice), coffee, and cooked eggs. Prepare two matching sets of scented samples by placing a small amount of each material in two opaque film canisters. Place a cotton ball over each sample to conceal its appearance without hiding its smell. Replace the lids on the canisters, labeling the bottoms of one set with numbers and the other set with letters. Keep a hidden record of the pairs that match. Place the sets on tables at opposite ends of the room. Instruct pairs of students to begin at one table and open one sample, smell it, and record its number (or letter). Then tell that pair to travel to the other table, smell each of the containers until it finds the matching scent and record the corresponding letter (or number). After a predetermined time, allow the pairs to compare their results with your answers.

Additional Multicultural Titles

Pueblo Boy: Growing Up In Two Worlds
Written and Photographed by Marcia Keegan
Published by Cobblehill Books

Flamboyan
Written by Arnold Adoff & Illustrated by Karen Barbour
Published by Harcourt Brace Jovanovich, Publishers

Sweet Clara And The Freedom Quilt
Written by Deborah Hopkinson & Illustrated by James Ransome
Published by Alfred A. Knopf, Inc.

The Princess And The Beggar: A Korean Folktale
Adapted and Illustrated by Anne Sibley O'Brien
Published by Scholastic Inc.

Kashtanka
Written by Anton Chekhov
Translated by Richard Pevear
Illustrated by Barry Moser
Published by The Putnam Publishing Group

The Day Of Ahmed's Secret
Written by Florence P. Heide
Published by Lothrop, Lee & Shepard Books

The Gift-Giver
Written by Joyce Hansen
Published by Houghton Mifflin Company

Today's Special: Z.A.P. & Zoe
Written by Athena V. Lord
Illustrated by Jean Jenkins
Published by Macmillan Children's Book Group

The Newbery Nook

Our Readers' Ideas For Using Newbery Books

Sounder, Leigh Botts, Maniac Magee, Mrs. Frisby—familiar names to many of your students. And what do they have in common? They're all found between the covers of Newbery Medal–winning books. Add a new page to your reading program with our subscribers' teacher-tested ideas for using Newbery books.

Background Information: The Newbery Medal

Awarded every year since 1922 for the finest children's book written by an American, the Newbery Medal is named after English bookseller and publisher John Newbery. This prestigious award is given annually by the Association for Library Service to Children of the American Library Association. Check with your school librarian for a list of Newbery Medal winners.

Bios And Book Jackets

I begin my favorite Newbery activity by sharing with students a little background information on both the Newbery and Caldecott awards. After previewing sample winners of each award, each student chooses a Newbery book. In addition to reading the book, the student researches and writes a short profile about the book's author. The student copies his proofread author profile on our computer; then he attaches it inside a book jacket that he has designed for the book. As a finishing touch, we decorate large, round gold stickers with a special class design; then we attach a sticker to the front of each book jacket. Finished book jackets are displayed in the library. *Sheri Leymeister—Gr. 5, Central Dauphin School District, Harrisburg, PA*

The Great Newbery Challenge

Try a fun group contest to familiarize students with Newbery books. Divide the class into pairs. Give each pair a list of Newbery books and a copy of the reproducible on page 41. Have each pair write its answers on a separate sheet of paper. After answers have been shared and checked, have each student who completed the sheet write his name on a small slip of paper. Place all of the slips in a jar; then draw two names. Award each lucky student a paperback copy of a recent Newbery winner. *Nancy Caudill—K–5 Librarian, Estes McDoniel Elementary, Henderson, NV*

Introducing Newbery Books

To introduce my new class of fourth graders to Newbery books, I surveyed the third-grade teachers to find out which Newbery titles they had read to the children the previous year. I covered a copy of each of these books with brown paper. In each I placed a bookmark at a section that would be instantly recognized by the students. As further preparation, I also selected several Newbery books with which students would probably be unfamiliar. In each book, I marked a short, attention-grabbing passage.

I began by showing students several Newbery books and explaining the history of the Newbery Medal. I then began reading the first covered book, *Caddie Woodlawn*. Immediately hands flew up in recognition! By the time we got to the fourth covered book, students were eager for more. I followed with eight short book talks on the unfamiliar Newbery winners. I closed the lesson by giving each student a duplicated list of Newbery winners, ready for that next trip to the library! *Alice T. Bull—Gr. K–4, Hamilton Elementary, Stroudsburg, PA*

The Newbery Reader Of The Day

Building enthusiasm for Newbery books is a snap with this simple tip. I set out a few Newbery books for students to preview. After looking through the books, the class selects the three titles that they would most like to have read aloud. Starting with the first choice, I let one child a day read a chapter aloud to the class. After reading, the student passes the book to the next reader so that she can prepare her chapter for the following day. (To keep track of readers, place a Post-it® note at the beginning of each chapter. On each note, write the name of the student who will be reading that particular chapter.) This easy-to-manage idea not only gets my students excited about Newbery books, but also guarantees that they are read to every day. *Betsy Combs—Gr. 5, Smithfield Elementary, Smithfield, NC*

Comparing Newbery Winners

Let students be the judge with this fun Newbery activity. I assign each child a specific year. The student's job is to read both the Newbery Medal book and the honor book for that year. After reading both books, the student writes a brief report comparing the two titles. In the report, he must tell whether or not he agrees with the judges' decision and must give reasons for his opinion. My students really enjoy reading these books and putting themselves in the judges' places. *Susan Barnett—Gr. 6, Roanoke Elementary, Fort Wayne, IN*

The "Bunch For Lunch" Newbery Club

To promote Newbery books at my school, I formed The "Bunch For Lunch" Newbery Club. Twenty-nine students signed up. Each month club members were instructed to read a specific Newbery winner or honor book during their free time. On the last Friday of the month, we met over lunch to discuss the book. Club members loved these luncheons/book discussions and became very proficient in expressing their opinions. In addition to the lunch and discussion, we completed a short activity based on each book. Some of the activities that we completed include:

- *Number The Stars:* Write a letter that might have been written by Annemarie to Ellen (or vice versa).
- *Dicey's Song:* Make a personality nametag for Dicey.
- *Hatchet:* Make a paper hatchet and label it with words to describe the courageous adventure.
- *The Family Under The Bridge:* Draw a large shopping cart and fill it with pictures of possessions that are important to you.

This yearlong activity was a favorite of my students and introduced them to wonderful books that they might never have cracked open. *Shelley Schultz—Gr. 6, J. W. P. Middle School, Waldorf, MN*

From The Mixed-up Files Of Mrs. Basil E. Frankweiler
written and illustrated by E. L. Konigsburg
published by Atheneum

- My students loved having the 1968 Newbery winner, *From The Mixed-up Files Of Mrs. Basil E. Frankweiler,* read to them. Since the book contained several illustrations, it was perfect for making a class display. First I enlarged each illustration on our copy machine; then I placed all of the pictures in a file. When I came to an illustrated page during reading, I awarded the enlarged version to a "great listener." That student was allowed to color the picture for the display. Finished pictures, accompanied by short captions, were posted on the wall in sequence. This visual record of the book helped absent students to catch up after missing part of the story. And the small reward motivated students to work on their listening skills. *Marilyn Davison—Gr. 5 & 6, River Oaks Elementary, Monroe, LA*

- *From The Mixed-up Files Of Mrs. Basil E. Frankweiler* is one of my students' favorites. The two main characters, Jamie and Claudia, are so colorfully described that I use the following idea to further explore their personalities. Two students volunteers (one boy and one girl) each lie on a large piece of butcher paper. After tracing their bodies and cutting out the tracings, the students decorate the cutouts to look like Claudia and Jamie. On the finished cutouts, students also write words to describe each character. We end up with a great display and a super workout on character development. *Patricia Shulman, Hillside Elementary, South Easton, MA*

Dear Mr. Henshaw
written by Beverly Cleary
illustrated by Paul O. Zelinsky
published by William Morrow And Company, Inc.

• After reading *Dear Mr. Henshaw,* each of my students followed Leigh's example by writing a letter to a favorite author. (Check with your librarian for a source of authors' or publishing companies' addresses.) When a student received a response from an author, I duplicated a copy of the letter, mounted it on construction paper, laminated it, and posted it on our "Authors Who Wrote Back" bulletin board. I also added a caption above each response telling which students wrote to that particular author. My students loved seeing their names associated with "their" authors. *Jean Herr—Gr. 5 & 6 Reading, Pawnee Elementary, Springfield, IL*

• Just as Leigh enjoyed writing a composition for the Young Writers' Yearbook, so my students relished the chance to do the same. Each child wrote an essay on a subject that we were studying in class. After revising their articles, students made final copies, which I then duplicated (one copy per student plus one extra). One copy of each essay was placed in a class "Young Writers' Yearbook," which we promptly placed in the school library. The remaining copies were bound together so that each student could have a personal copy of the yearbook to take home. *Jill Barnett—Gr. 4 & 5, Anderson Community Schools, Anderson, IN*

• Sprinkled liberally throughout *Dear Mr. Henshaw* are many suggestions on how to be a good writer. As your class reads the book, keep a running list of the tips on a large piece of chart paper. You'll wind up with a handy reference chart that students will really pay attention to during your own writers' workshop! *Karen E. Brege, Kenmore Middle School, Buffalo, NY*

• As Leigh's attitude worsens, the school janitor takes notice and states, "SO you've got problems…." As a whole-class or small-group activity, have students list Leigh's problems as you read. When the list is complete, have students rank the problems in order from least serious to most serious. Extend this activity by having each child list and rank problems that he is having in his journal. Be sure to respond to each child's list by writing a message back to him in the journal. *Janet Smith—Gr. 5, Meade Memorial Elementary, Williamsport, KY*

The Westing Game
written and illustrated by Ellen Raskin
published by Dutton Children's Books

• Filled with mind-boggling clues and characters, *The Westing Game* is a popular favorite with my sixth graders. To help students keep the assorted clues and characters straight, we created an interesting display. As the game partners and their clues were revealed, we posted them on the board (see the illustration). The display really helped alleviate confusion when clues were referred to or theories were formed by characters in the book. Students even used the bulletin board to make their own predictions. My class loved this book so much that I reread many sections by popular demand right before summer vacation! *Marilyn Davison—Gr. 5 & 6, River Oaks Elementary, Monroe, LA*

Partners

Turtle Wexler (witch)	**+**	Flora Baumbach (dressmaker)

Grace Windsor Wexler (heiress)	**+**	James Shin Hoo (restaurateur)

Clues

sea	mountain
am	O

fruited	purple
waves	for	sea

Number The Stars
written by Lois Lowry
published by Houghton Mifflin Company

• The 1990 Newbery Medal winner, *Number The Stars,* is a great addition to a unit on World War II. In November we read the book during our reading period and studied World War II in social studies class. We also invited two former World War II prisoners of war to speak to us the day after Veterans Day. Students talked about this unit for the rest of the year! *Julie Hagedorn—Gr. 5, Oscar-Howe Elementary, Sioux Falls, SD*

Name _____

The Newbery Medal Challenge

Use a list of Newbery Medal books to answer the following questions. Write your answers on another sheet of paper.

1. What book won the first Newbery Medal? In what year?

2. What book won the most recent Newbery Medal? In what year?

3. List each Newbery book that begins with the word *A* (for example, *A Wrinkle In Time).*

4. List each Newbery book that has one of the following words in its title: *Mr., Mrs., Miss, Mister.*

5. List each Newbery book that has at least one comma in its title.

6. List each Newbery book that has an apostrophe in its title.

7. List each Newbery book that begins with the word *The.*

8. List each Newbery book that has only two words in its title.

9. List each Newbery book that has only three words in its title.

©1998 The Education Center, Inc. • *The Best Of* The Mailbox® *Literature* • *Intermediate* • TEC1464 • Nancy Caudill—K–5 Librarian, Estes McDoniel Elementary, Henderson, NV • Key p. 160

Note To The Teacher: Use with "The Great Newbery Challenge" on page 38.

Pass The Poetry, Please!

In today's classroom, poetry is a vital ingredient to improving literacy and encouraging a love of writing and reading. Instead of limiting your use of poetry to a three-week unit that kids will soon forget, enjoy it all year long with the following creative activities.

with contributions by
Nancy Lorenz—Grs. 5 & 6, Chicago, IL

Introducing Poetry

Kids are often hesitant about both reading and writing poetry. You can help students overcome their fears and prejudices by easing them into poetry and modeling enthusiasm for it. Start early in the school year by reading several poems from *Reflections On A Gift Of Watermelon Pickle And Other Modern Verse* edited by Stephen Dunning. Each poem describes a familiar item without naming it. After sharing a poem, have students guess what it is describing. Next share some humorous poems from collections such as *For Laughing Out Loud: Poems To Tickle Your Funny Bone* selected by Jack Prelutsky, *Fresh Brats* by X. J. Kennedy, or *Nonstop Nonsense* by Margaret Mahy. Finally, share one or two of your favorite poems. Explain why you like each poem and invite students to give their reactions. Announce that poetry will play a big part in the upcoming school year; then have each student use a glitter pen or other fancy writing instrument to sign a colorful "Poetry Has A Place Here!" banner. Hang the banner in a prominent spot in your classroom.

42

Poetry Pot

For an easy and fun introduction to writing poetry, duplicate the cards on pages 47 and 48 on construction paper. Laminate the cards before cutting them out; then place them in a large pot or other container. Have a volunteer pull out ten cards. List the cards' words and phrases on the chalkboard; then have students as a class arrange them to create an original poem. Write the poem on a piece of chart paper as students dictate it. Repeat this exercise until students seem comfortable with the process.

Next have the class sit in a circle on the floor. Give each student a piece of art paper; then pass the pot around the circle, instructing each child to remove six to ten cards. Have the child manipulate the cards on her paper to create an original poem. Reassure students that rhyming isn't necessary; nor do they have to worry about making complete sentences or thoughts. Allow students to trade cards, return cards to the pot, or draw additional cards until they are satisfied with their poems. After writing, illustrating, and sharing his poem, have each child make a construction-paper journal in which he lists interesting words or phrases to use in future poems. Encourage students to gather entries from current units of study, books they're reading, personal experiences, etc. Set aside ten minutes each week for students to meet in small groups to swap ideas for their journals.

Cooperative Group Anthologies

To build an appreciation for all types of poetry, have cooperative groups work together to create poetry anthologies. Ask your media specialist for help in gathering a collection of good poetry books. (See our suggestions on pages 44 and 45.) Divide students into several cooperative groups. As a class, discuss criteria students might set for evaluating poetry: rhythm, imagery, humor, rhyme, shape, etc. List the criteria on a piece of chart paper displayed in the classroom; then tell students that during the next two weeks, each group will be creating its own poetry anthology.

Give each group a copy of the reproducible chart on page 46 to use in planning its anthology. Set aside a week for groups to read the books and choose their favorite poems. The next week have students copy and illustrate each poem to be included in their anthologies. Have each group add a table of contents and a cover to its anthology, as well as a group article explaining why the particular poems were selected. Display the finished anthologies in your media center. For fun, have each group select one of its poems to present as a choral reading to the rest of the class.

Pam Crane

Poetry Every Day

Making poetry a part of every day isn't as hard as it sounds if you follow these tips:

- Use thematic collections of poetry to introduce science or social studies units. For example, use *Earth Songs* by Myra Cohn Livingston to supplement a unit on geology or environmental studies.
- Each week, have one student copy a favorite poem on a large piece of chart paper. Post the poem on a bulletin board. During the week, have each student write his reaction to the poem on an index card to post on the bulletin board.
- At any time during the day, allow a student to call for a "poetry freeze." During this time, everyone stops what he's doing and listens to a poem. For fun, let students call for a freeze during gym or while quietly walking down the hallway.
- Keep several favorite anthologies on your desk. Each day pick a poem to share with students.
- Periodically have students respond to journal topics using poetry instead of prose.
- Give a cooperative group a copy of a poem. Give the group ten minutes to plan a dramatization of the poem to share with the class.

I've Got The Poetry Jitters!

Your students may be nervous about their first poetry-writing experience. Calm jitters with these terrific starter ideas:

- Choose an emotion and a color you think symbolizes that emotion. Use the following model to write an original poem:

(An emotion) seems (a color).	Loneliness seems golden yellow.
Like (a comparison).	Like the hazy colors fall days bring.
I see _____.	I see leaves of red and orange.
I hear _____.	I hear birds announce themselves.
I smell _____.	I smell burning leaves that signal the end of something.
I touch _____.	I touch no one for I am alone.
I taste _____.	I taste the salt of my tears.

- Use your name and the following model to express thoughts about yourself:

(Name of child), (a descriptive phrase),	Jason, a rambunctious fellow,
Who feels...	Who feels silly.
Who needs...	Who needs everyone to laugh.
Who gives...	Who gives not a clue to his feelings.
Who fears...	Who fears no one will like him.
Who would like to...	Who would like to take a vacation.

- Begin a poem with the words "I do not understand." List three things you don't understand about the world, yourself, or other people. These can be important, serious, or silly things. Then name the thing you don't understand the most. End with something you do understand.

I do not understand why people are starving.
I do not understand why no one will help.
I do not understand why children aren't being fed.
But most of all, I do not understand why three can't be friends.
I do understand that life is sometimes confusing.

Outstanding Poetry Collections

reviewed by Deborah Zink Roffino

Brown Honey In Broomwheat Tea

written by Joyce Carol Thomas
illustrated by Floyd Cooper
published by HarperCollins Children's Books, 1993

Lines of free verse swirl about the pages of this moving collection that glorifies the beauty of an African-American heritage. Rustic colors glow on the pages as a young girl views herself through the eyes of her family. A call to cherish our own heritage and celebrate who we are permeates these dramatic verses.

The Tamarindo Puppy And Other Poems

written by Charlotte Pomerantz
illustrated by Byron Barton
published by Greenwillow Books, 1993

Two languages—English and Spanish—flow easily throughout this collection *and* off the tongue of the reader. A change of language in a line of a poem never slows the pace; rather, the repetition becomes a device to teach another language. Bright, happy illustrations are the perfect complement to Pomerantz's energetic poems.

Pass It On: African-American Poetry For Children

selected by Wade Hudson and illustrated by Floyd Cooper
published by Scholastic Inc., 1993

Gathered on these rich pages are works by Nikki Giovanni, Gwendolyn Brooks, Lucille Clifton, Langston Hughes, and 12 other gifted poets. Pride, love, innocence, and jubilation are wrapped together in a poetry collection that introduces children to the works of some of our most outstanding African-American writers.

Not A Copper Penny In Me House: Poems From The Caribbean

written by Monica Gunning and illustrated by Frané Lessac
published by Wordsong/Boyds Mills Press, 1993

Follow a Jamaican youngster through the lively routines of her daily life in the Caribbean. The vivid verses—detailing the architecture, education, language, marketplaces, lazy Sundays, and wild weather of the Caribbean—are the next best thing to visiting the tropical islands. Gunning's descriptive poems from a child's point of view offer intriguing glimpses into island life.

Night On A Neighborhood Street

written by Eloise Greenfield
illustrated by Jan Spivey Gilchrist
published by Dial Books For Young Readers, 1991

Familiar faces, soothing, ordinary sounds, well-worn paths—that's what makes a neighborhood. These traditional and free-verse poems take a few unexceptional moments and make them unforgettable. In this lovely collection, award-winning poet Eloise Greenfield uses her poems to urge children to reexamine that which they thought was commonplace.

The Trees Stand Shining: Poetry Of The North American Indians

selected by Hettie Jones
illustrated by Robert Andrew Parker
published by Dial Books, 1993

Short, stunning verses softly hold the heart of the reader in this collection of Native American poetry. Originally songs taught to Native American children, these beautiful lyrics glorify nature and a close relationship with the earth. The nearly impressionistic paintings of Robert Andrew Parker set a dramatic mood for these fine poems.

Festival In My Heart: Poems By Japanese Children

selected and translated by Bruno Navasky
published by Harry N. Abrams, Inc.; 1993

Originally printed as a daily feature in Japan's leading newspaper, these poems by Japanese elementary schoolchildren provide an unforgettable glimpse into another culture. Although written by children who live halfway around the world, the sweet surprise of this collection is the number of yearnings and emotions common to all kids: a love of nature, a lonely ache for a parent, scary dreams, despair over teasing. Spectacular artwork further displays the Japanese culture.

At The Crack Of The Bat

selected by Lillian Morrison
illustrated by Steve Cieslawski
published by Hyperion Books For Children, 1992

Like ghosts from empty ballparks, this superior anthology is full of shadows from a time before free agents and multimillion-dollar contracts. The draw of the game was the crack of the bat, the dust on the cleats, the hammering of the plate. For those less versed in baseball history, there is an epilogue with a brief explanation of each poem.

Ring Out, Wild Bells: Poems About Holidays And Seasons

selected by Lee Bennett Hopkins
illustrated by Karen Baumann
published by Harcourt Brace Jovanovich, 1992

The glory of every season, every holiday, every special occasion is celebrated in this jam-packed anthology. Where else can you find a joyful ode to Groundhog Day, Columbus Day, or May Day? Christina Rossetti, Carl Sandburg, Langston Hughes, and Robert Frost are all here with scores of other poets. This superb collection is for all children, every day of the year.

Eats

written by Arnold Adoff and illustrated by Susan Russo
published by Mulberry Books, 1992

The sweet smells of the kitchen and the rich fragrance of the garden waft off each page of this collection of flowing free verse. Whether it's tea or toast, spaghetti or strawberries, Adoff makes young readers discover the hidden details to be found in the most ordinary "eats."

The Dragons Are Singing Tonight

written by Jack Prelutsky and illustrated by Peter Sis
published by Greenwillow Books, 1993

Do you believe in dragons? You just might after reading this magical collection by popular poet Jack Prelutsky. From silly, singsong verses to infectious rhymes that appeal to all ages, this charming collection is full of fantastic creatures that will spark even the most timid imagination.

Other Recommended Collections

- *Extra Innings: Baseball Poems*
  selected by Lee Bennett Hopkins
  Harcourt Brace Jovanovich, 1993

- *Out Of The Blue: Poems About Color*
  by Hiawyn Oram
  Hyperion Books For Children, 1993

- *Dragon Poems*
  selected by John Foster and Korky Paul
  Oxford University Press, 1991

- *Chortles: New And Selected Wordplay Poems*
  by Eve Merriam
  Morrow Junior Books, 1989

- *All The Colors Of The Race*
  by Arnold Adoff
  Lothrop, Lee & Shepard, 1982

- *Something Big Has Been Here*
  by Jack Prelutsky
  Greenwillow Books, 1990

- *Roomrimes*
  by Sylvia Cassedy
  HarperCollins, 1987

- *All The Small Poems*
  by Valerie Worth
  Farrar, Straus & Giroux, Inc.; 1987

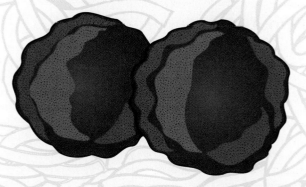

Planning A Group Poetry Anthology

As you read poetry books with your group, decide on ten or more poems to include in an original anthology. Fill out this planning chart as you work. Use it to complete your anthology. Remember to select poems on a variety of topics and written by different poets. Use the back of this page if you need more space.

Title of poem	Taken from (title of book)	Author of poem	Reason(s) for including in anthology

Title of our anthology: _____

Table of contents
to be completed by _____
group member(s)

Anthology due date: _____
Cover to be designed
and completed by _____
group member(s)

©1998 The Education Center, Inc. • The Best Of The Mailbox® Literature • Intermediate • TEC1464

Note To The Teacher: Use with "Cooperative Group Anthologies" on page 42.

dusty	being impatient	the color of potatoes	ruby red
under the desk	nibbling	on the edge	do you have
brushing	tangled	quickly	skipping breakfast
rubbery	brontosaurus	impossible to	gazing at
hooves	dozens of	a traveler	climbing steadily
from here	storyteller	flour	big hungry bear
thinking about	anxiously	trust	hut
tickled	beard	frightening things	inside the barn
baggy shorts	sneakers	mural	thinking
thundering	a stack of	early morning	not now
small secrets	imagine	serenading	confusion
remember this	racing	made of dreams	next to
ridiculous	fighting for	I never thought	if only
ribbons	mice	yelped	teeth
sighing	twinkling eyes	grandparents	freckles
tapping noises	what do you do with	I give	chewing gum
towering skyscrapers	plink	once	I think about
bothers	the basement	beat the drums	an accident
long ago	war and peace	castle	cheering crowds
counting the minutes	skiing	puppet	time to
investigated	windy	shocking	planet
falling raindrops	clubhouse	dunking	zebras
bending	scales	thumbprint	on the highway
free	of life	chocolate sundae	crocodile skin
all arms	woolly	slither	gentle

toad	bouquet	prizewinner	incandescent
arrow soaring	rainbow in the sky	bed of leaves	honking
sneakily spying	ladybug	fluttering	neon
sticky sweet	blotchy	pencil	flamingo
hear ye	it's for you	papery	surprise
clink of coins	yard sale	rub-a-dub	chocolate cake
garbage	apple seeds	zip	on the street
rooftop	trophy	pebbles on the porch	broccoli
my neighbors	hatchet	heartaches	loud celebrations
hop along	deep blues	brothers	rap
fingernails	crowded	cuddled	cast a vote
gobbled	blur	zoom	pumpkin pie
plenty of it	crimson	never mind	soda pop
shimmering shine	innocent	crushing	runny
goofy	fluffed	in the evening	dripping ice cream
tart	fog	plopping	water bugs
galloping	I love	but why	don't forget
fire-breathing	like a bat	dirt	peeling
odor	run away	upside down	fish fins
gigantic	sharks	sparkling	know the plan
in purple hats	herd of	blowing whistle	six feet tall
a new year	but not now	busy	noodles
dashing	a long time ago	silver snowflakes	blankets
smoke in our	not really red	meanest	river
rapidly losing my	aloha	amigo	nervously waiting

What A Great Ending!

A Novel Way To End Your Reading Program

It's the end of the year—a frantic time of field trips, art fairs, awards' programs, and achievement tests all squeezed into a few short weeks. With all the interruptions in your normal class routine, does starting that last end-of-the-year novel seem like a chore? It doesn't have to anymore! Try this end-of-the-year idea—a proven success for one of our readers—for a great close to your reading program.

*adapted from an idea by
Jackie Sandoz, Mandeville, LA*

Pam Crane

A Novel End To A Great Year

Instead of reading the same novel together as a class—a difficult task with all the interruptions that characterize the final days of a school year—let each student select a book of his own to read. Then encourage your students to complete a variety of stimulating activities on their books. Here's how the activity works:

- During the first 15 minutes of reading class, teach a mini skill lesson. At this point in the year, you'll probably want to spend time reviewing important reading skills.
- During the next 20–25 minutes, have students read silently from the books they've selected.
- For the last 20–25 minutes of class, have students work independently on the book activities listed on page 51.

Have students turn in their completed projects as they're done so that evaluating the work isn't an overwhelming task. While students read silently and work on the activities, you can be available to answer questions and hold one-on-one conferences with students who need extra guidance or feedback. Set aside a final day during which students share about their books and favorite activities.

How Do I Get Started?

1. Compile a list of great books suitable for your students' interests and reading abilities. Or duplicate the list we've provided on page 50 for each child. Half of the list includes titles of outstanding children's fiction. The other half lists noted authors. Have each child select either a book to read from the left column or an author from the right column. If a student selects an author, have him work with your school's media specialist to select an appropriate book by the author.

2. Make one copy of the book-activities contract on page 51. Decide on the number of unstarred activities you want each child to complete. Fill in that number on the copy along with a due date; then duplicate the contract for each student. Have each student staple his contract inside a folder in which he can store his work.

3. Duplicate student copies of the reproducibles on pages 52–55. Store the class set of each page in a labeled file folder; then place these folders at a reading center where they will be easily accessible to students. At the center, place other materials students will need to complete the activities.

49

Choose A Novel

Pick one; then head to the library
to find the book and identify its author.

Hatchet

The Twenty-One Balloons

Matilda

The Search For Delicious

Night Of the Twisters

Old Yeller

Missing May

On My Honor

Shiloh

The Midwife's Apprentice

Summer Of The Monkeys

Dicey's Song

Who Comes With Cannons?

Skinnybones

Nothing But The Truth

An Occasional Cow

Rasco And The Rats Of NIMH

Harriet The Spy

Stinker From Space

Afternoon Of The Elves

The Land I Lost

Journey To America

The House Of Dies Drear

The Cay

Roll Of Thunder, Hear My Cry

Stepping On The Cracks

The Borrowers

Bridge To Terabithia

The Boggart

Sixth Grade Can Really Kill You

Choose An Author

Pick one; then head to the library
to find a book written by your author.

Gary Paulsen

Barthe DeClements

Roald Dahl

Natalie Babbitt

Pam Conrad

Cynthia Rylant

Jerry Spinelli

Louis Sachar

Phyllis Reynolds Naylor

Dick King-Smith

Betsy Byars

Paula Danziger

Jean Craighead George

Lois Lowry

Robert N. Peck

Katherine Paterson

Madeleine L'Engle

Paula Fox

Scott O'Dell

E. L. Konigsburg

Cynthia Voight

Mildred D. Taylor

Virginia Hamilton

Walter Dean Myers

Patricia MacLachlan

Jean Van Leeuwen

Lucy M. Montgomery

Lynne Reid Banks

Bill Brittain

Lloyd Alexander

Don't You Just <u>Love</u> A Good Ending?

The school year is ending—and what better way to celebrate a great year than by reading a great book? Work on these activities as you read and after you finish your book. Complete one starred (*) activity and _____ other activities by _____.

due date

Title of my book: _____

Author: _____

Of Flamingos And Friends

Summarize each chapter and write a prediction for the next chapter in your journal.

Complete the "A 'Patch-word' Quilt" activity.

★ On a large index card, design a travel postcard that illustrates the setting of your book. On the back, write a message from a main character to you.

Complete the "Keys To A Character" activity.

Write a newspaper article that describes the main event in your book.

Draw a Venn diagram that compares this book with another we have read in class this year.

Complete the "Here's The Scoop On My Book!" activity.

★ Draw a design of a new product that could have been created by your book's main character. Label the product and add a caption telling why it was created.

Complete the " 'Hand-ling' Conflict" activity.

★ Cut out words and pictures that relate to your book from old magazines. Glue them onto a piece of construction paper to make a collage.

Complete the "Step-By-Step Story Map" activity.

Create a ten-item quiz on your book. Attach an answer key to your quiz.

Note To The Teacher: Use with the reading activity described on page 49, and with the reproducibles on pages 52–55. Fill in the two blanks in the student directions before duplicating.

Name _____

A "Patch-word" Quilt

Follow these simple steps to build a class "patch-word" quilt as you read your book.

1. Write your name and your book's title and author on any patch on the quilt.
2. When you come to a word you don't know, copy its sentence in your journal. Then write what you think the word means. Check a dictionary and revise your definition if necessary. Then write the word in black marker on a numbered patch below.
3. When all the patches have been labeled, color them according to this code: *noun* = red; *verb* = green; *adjective* = yellow; *adverb* = blue. Cut out the quilt with pinking shears and give it to your teacher.

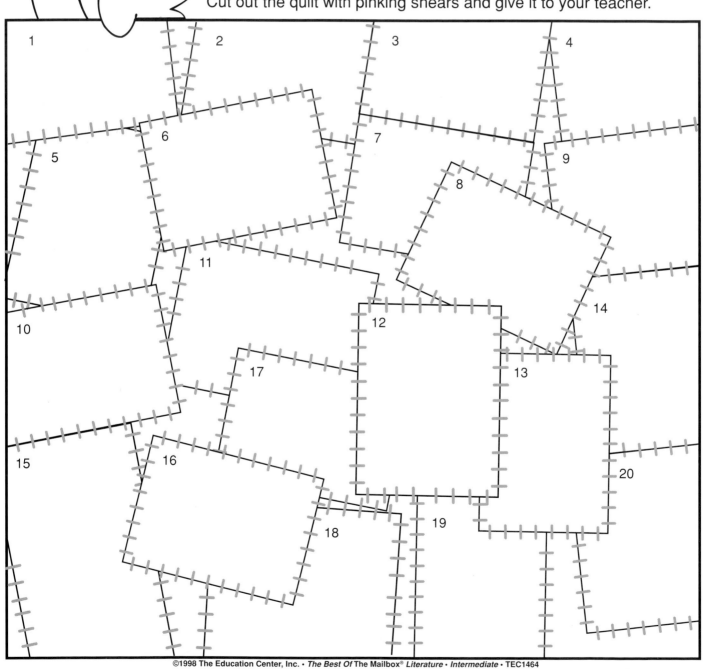

Note To The Teacher: Cover a bulletin board with background paper and title it "Our 'Patch-word' Quilt." Be sure each student has a journal in which to do his work and a black marker. Also provide a pair of pinking shears. Staple students' cut-out patterns in grid fashion on the board to create a class quilt of words. Duplicate extra copies of this page for any student who wishes to complete more than one pattern for his book.

Name _____

Step-By-Step Story Map

Fill in the boxes to complete a story map about your book.

Title: _____

Author: _____

Setting: _____

Event: _____

Event: _____

Problem: _____

Characters: _____

Event: _____

Climax (Turning Point): _____

Conclusion: _____

Note To The Teacher: Use with the contract on page 51.

Keys To A Character

Ready to unlock the mystery behind a favorite character in your book? First fill in the blanks below. Next fill in the keys with words or phrases that describe the physical and personality traits of your character. Then, on the back of this page, write the answers to the key questions in the box.

Title of book: _____

Author: _____ Character: _____

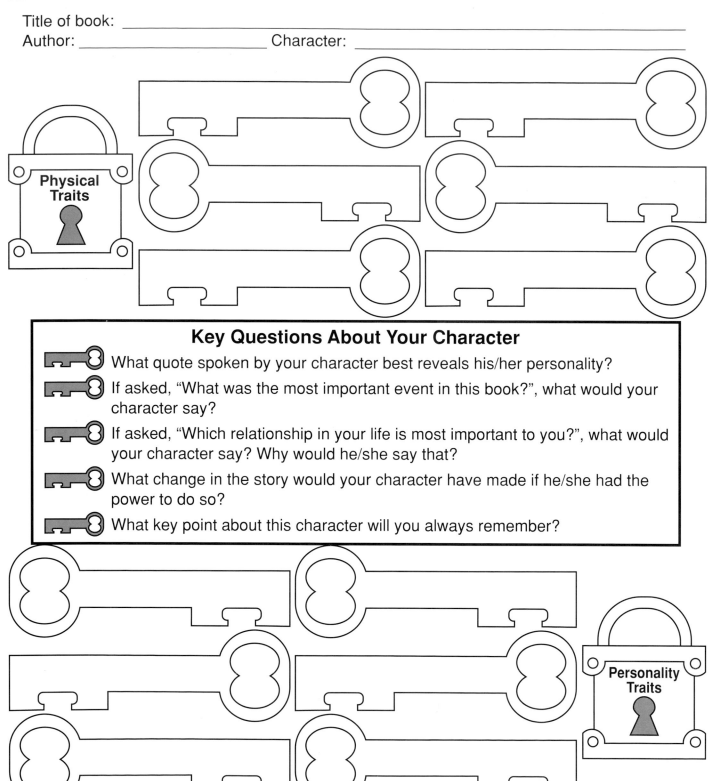

Key Questions About Your Character

What quote spoken by your character best reveals his/her personality?

If asked, "What was the most important event in this book?", what would your character say?

If asked, "Which relationship in your life is most important to you?", what would your character say? Why would he/she say that?

What change in the story would your character have made if he/she had the power to do so?

What key point about this character will you always remember?

"Hand-ling" Conflict

How did the main character in your book handle conflict? For each of the conflicts this character faced (see the list of four choices below), trace one of your hands on a sheet of colored paper. Cut out the tracings. Then follow the directions for labeling each hand cutout.

If your character had a conflict with...

- **another character in the book:** Label the thumb of one hand cutout with the name of the other character. On the palm of the cutout, describe an example of the struggle.

- **nature (storms, wilderness, etc.):** Label the thumb of another hand cutout "Nature." On the palm, describe an example of the struggle.

- **rules, laws, or customs:** Label the thumb of a hand cutout "Rules." On the palm, describe an example of the struggle.

- **himself/herself:** Label the thumb of another hand cutout with the character's name. On the palm, describe how the character struggled with himself/herself.

Next make a poster about the conflicts in your book by gluing your hand cutouts onto a large sheet of paper. Title the poster; then add any drawings or captions that you'd like. Display the poster for your classmates to see.

How
Sal Hiddle
"Hand-led"
Conflict

Rules
Nature
Sal
Mrs. Cadaver

©1998 The Education Center, Inc. • *The Best Of The Mailbox® Literature • Intermediate* • TEC1464

Note To The Teacher: Use this sheet with the contract on page 51. Provide each student with several sheets of light-colored construction paper, fine-tipped markers, scissors, glue, and a poster-sized sheet of paper.

Here's The Scoop On My Book!

Answer at least seven of these questions on your own paper. After you answer a question, color its scoop of ice cream. When you're finished, staple this sheet on top of your answer sheet.

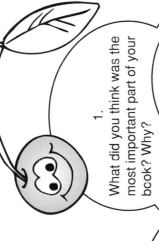

1. What did you think was the most important part of your book? Why?

2. Which part of the story did you visualize (see in your mind) most clearly? Describe the details as you imagined them.

3. Which character did you like the best? Why?

4. Which character did you like the least? Why?

5. At what point in the book were you sure you knew the outcome? Why?

6. Did you like the outcome of the story? Why or why not?

7. Were there any loose ends in this story that were not tied up to your satisfaction? Describe them.

8. What other story does this book remind you of? Why?

9. Would this story make a good movie? Why or why not?

10. What do you think was the theme or moral of this book?

Book Title: _____
Author: _____

©1998 The Education Center, Inc. • *The Best Of The Mailbox® Literature • Intermediate* • TEC1464

Note To The Teacher: Use this sheet with the contract on page 51.

Books Make Summer

A Reading Incentive Program For The End Of The Year (Or anytime!)

As summer vacation nears, books are probably the last thing on your students' minds. So pack the following reading incentive program into those final weeks of school. Then don't be surprised when your most reluctant reader waves good-bye with the words, "Mind if I borrow this book for the summer?"

by Diana Willis

Use It Now Or Use It Later

Don't let the title of this unit fool you—the motivating activities and reproducibles that follow can be used at any time of the school year. If you plan on using the activities at the end of the year, you'll want to spend a minimum of four weeks on the unit. This will give you plenty of time to build interest and give your students time to reach some reading goals before heading home for the summer.

Want to save this program for next year? No problem! Change the unit title to "A 'Bear-y' Special Start" and use the activities as a back-to-school introduction to reading. Or use the title "Bear With Us—We're Reading!" and incorporate the activities into your celebration of National Children's Book Week in November or Reading Is Fun Week in April. Whenever you decide to use these fun activities, your students will "bear-ly" be able to contain their reenergized excitement about books!

A "Bear-y" Special Start

What better way to get students excited about reading than by reading to them! A couple of weeks before introducing the unit, spend time each day reading a terrific summer book such as *Summer Of The Monkeys* by Wilson Rawls or *Jelly Belly* by Robert Kimmel Smith. *Summer Of The Monkeys* is a delightful novel about a mountain boy who encounters hilarious problems when he tries to recapture a troop of escaped circus monkeys. With humor and sensitivity, *Jelly Belly* tells the story of Ned, a boy who must spend his summer at Camp Lean-Too, a camp for overweight children. On the last day of reading, introduce the unit and give children their suitcase patterns and reading record sheets on pages 59 and 60 (see ideas that follow).

Packing My Bag With Books!

For an appealing bulletin board that "bear-ly" takes any time to complete, try this motivating display. Cut out a bear pattern; then post it on a bulletin board with the title "Reading Makes Summer 'Bear-able' " or "Books Are 'Bear' Necessities Of Life!" Then duplicate the suitcase pattern on page 59 on white construction paper for each child. Have each student write his name on the luggage tag, then color (leaving the travel patches uncolored) and cut out his suitcase. Post all the students' suitcases on the board. When a student reads a book, have him write its title and author on one of his patches. Encourage each child to fill in at least one patch before summer vacation begins. Send the suitcases home on the last day of school as reminders to "paws" to read this summer!

"Bear-able"!

A "Bear Necessities" Reading Record

After completing the bulletin-board activity, give each student a copy of the reading record on page 60. Whenever a child completes a book, have her fill out one of the suitcases on her record. Provide time each morning for informal book talks by students who wish to share books they've just finished. Use the award/book list on page 58 to recognize students who meet reading goals or make outstanding progress. If using the unit at the end of the year, give each child an additional record sheet to take home with the challenge to make reading a "bear-y" special part of summer vacation.

A Honey Of A Song

Even intermediate kids like belting out a favorite tune! To get your reading program off to a smashing start, teach your students the following song (see the melody below). Sing the first line of verse one; then have students repeat it. Continue with the remaining three phrases, after which everyone sings the entire verse together as the chorus. Repeat for the remaining verses.

Lyrics

The other day *(students repeat)*
I met a bear, *(students repeat)*
Up in the woods *(students repeat)*
A way up there. *(students repeat)*
CHORUS

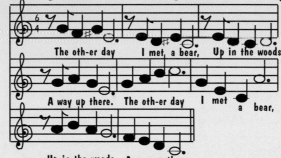

He looked at me; I looked at him.
He sized me up; I sized up him.

That grizzly bear then grinned at me
When he saw my book beneath the tree.

He said to me, "Why don't you run?
I see you ain't got any gun!"

You bet I ran away from there
But right behind me was that bear!

And so I jumped into the air
But missed that branch, a way up there!

Now, don't you fret, now, don't you frown!
I caught that branch on the way back down!

When I looked down—oh, glory be!
That bear, he sat beneath the tree.

Would you believe? (And this is true!)
He read my book the whole way through!

And then he left, and I climbed down.
A friendly bear, I must have found.

As you can see, that book saved me.
I love to read—oh, lucky me!

I bet you've guessed this story's done
Until I read another one!

My Hunger For Books Is "Un-bear-able"!

During the course of your reading program, be sure to schedule daily times of SSR (Sustained Silent Reading). Let students grab their books and head to comfortable spots in the room to plop down and read. At the end of one of these sessions, surprise your kids with a snack that even a hungry bear would be pleased with! Serve teddy bear-shaped cookies or peanut butter sandwiches. Treat hungry readers to small paper cups of Teddy Grahams® or Gummi Bears.

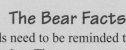

The Bear Facts

Sometimes kids need to be reminded that good books don't just mean fiction. There are many outstanding nonfiction books that can easily capture an intermediate student's attention. To make your class more aware of nonfiction books, try this fun project. Draw a bear pattern similar to the one shown. For each student, duplicate two to four copies of the pattern on light-colored construction paper. After students have cut out their bears, head to the library! Challenge each child to look through nonfiction books and magazines to find interesting and unusual facts. The student writes each fact in her own words on one of the bear patterns, listing the source from which the information was taken on the back of the pattern. After sharing the facts back in the classroom, have students post them as an attractive border around your bulletin board (see "Packing My Bag With Books" on page 56). Keep these fascinating facts handy for future classes by laminating them.

If you were a frontier child, you'd have to give your dad whatever money you earned until you turned 21 years old. That was the law!

Matt

The "Books Are 'Bear' Necessities" Award

Given to:

_____

For: _____

_____

Signed: _____   **Date:** _____

Ready for more "un-bear-ably" terrific books? Try one of these!

Fiction

The Bears' House by Marilyn Sachs
Fantastic Mr. Fox by Roald Dahl
And Nobody Knew They Were There by Otto Salassi
North To Freedom by Anne Holm
Skinnybones by Barbara Park

Nonfiction

Homesick: My Own Story by Jean Fritz
The President's Car by Nancy Winslow Parker
The Price Of Free Land by Treva Adams Strait
How Things Work by Neil Ardley
Jambo Means Hello by Muriel Feelings

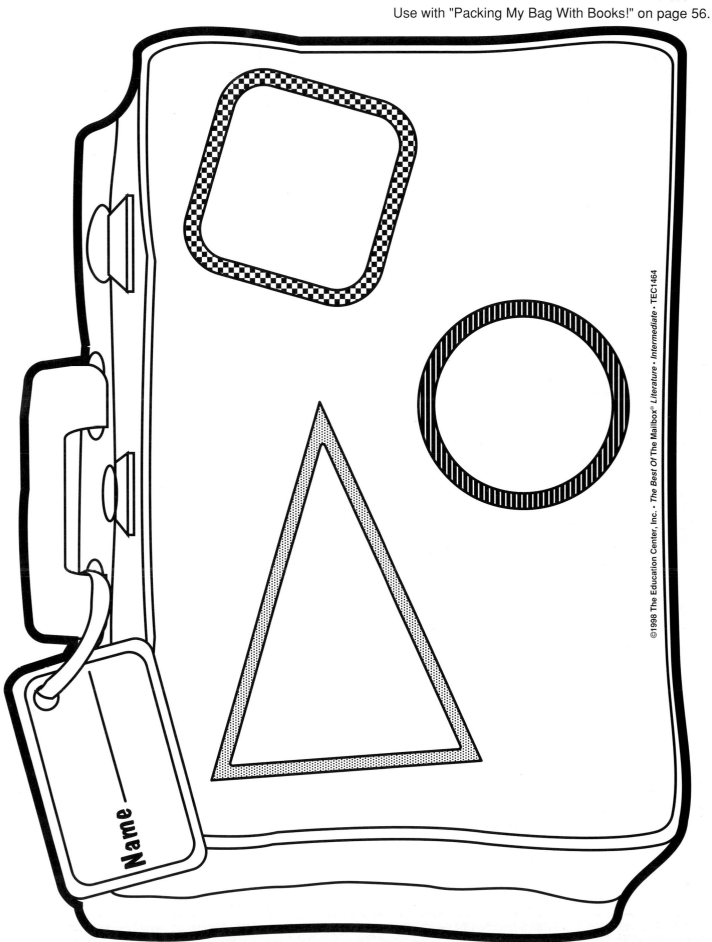

Name

©1998 The Education Center, Inc. • *The Best Of* The Mailbox® *Literature* • *Intermediate* • TEC1464

Reading record sheet

Name ______________________

I'm Packing My Bags With Books!

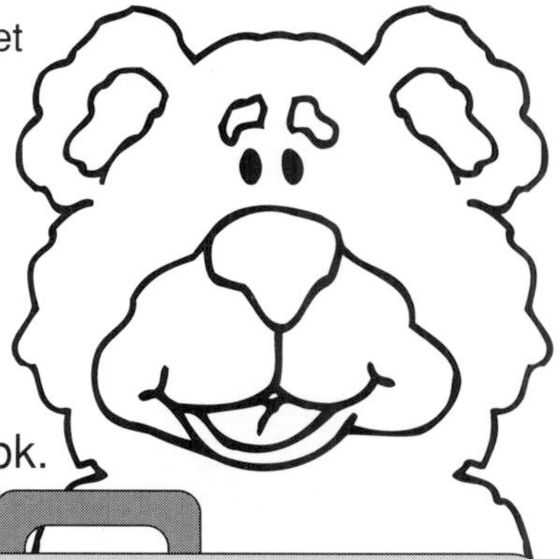

Fill in and lightly color a suitcase each time you finish a book.

Title: ______________________
____
Author: ______________________
____

Title: ______________________
____
Author: ______________________
____

Title: ______________________
____
Author: ______________________
____

Title: ______________________
____
Author: ______________________
____

Title: ______________________
____
Author: ______________________
____

Title: ______________________
____
Author: ______________________
____

Title: ______________________
____
Author: ______________________
____

Title: ______________________
____
Author: ______________________
____

Title: ______________________
____
Author: ______________________
____

Novel Units

Delve deeper into your favorite novels with units that make it easy and fun to teach basic skills, integrate your curriculum, incorporate hands-on learning, and expand your students' critical-thinking abilities.

The Great BRAIN

A Children's Favorite
by John D. Fitzgerald

Meet Thomas Dennis Fitzgerald—"The Great Brain" of Adenville, Utah. Admired by his brothers, J. D. and Sweyn, for his intellectual prowess, Tom could outsmart most adults and turn any situation into a profitable enterprise— usually to his own advantage! Share this lively, touching book with your students; then extend their reading experience with the following creative ideas and reproducibles.

by Mary Anne T. Haffner and Sue Ireland

Somehow Tom (known as T. D.) convinces his little brother, J. D., that certain situations call for loyalty and silence. Divide students into two groups to debate the issue of whether or not it is ever justifiable to "tattle." Let each side speak for three to five minutes. Encourage students to relate situations in which they have had to decide whether or not to "tell on someone." After all arguments have been heard, culminate what was probably a very lively discussion by having students write persuasive paragraphs stating their personal opinions.

ADENVILLE *WEEKLY ADVOCATE*

J.D. GETS MUMPS FIRST!
Noteworthy News

The Fitzgerald boys' father was editor and publisher of the local newspaper, the *Adenville Weekly Advocate*. Have students pretend that they are reporters working for the newspaper. Their assignment is to write stories for the following headlines. Remind each "cub reporter" to inclue the five W's in his story: *Who? What? When? Where?* and *Why?*

- First Water Closet Installed In Adenville
- The Traveling Emporium Comes To Town
- J. D. Get Mumps First
- Brothers Lost In Skeleton Cave! The Great Brain Saves The Day!
- Adenville Schoolteacher Reinstated
- The Great Brain Rescues Andy Anderson

Looking Back To 1896

With the story set in 1896, the Fitzgerald boys grew up in a world far different from that of today's youngsters. Ask your librarian to help you gather a collection of resources on the Gay Nineties. Form research teams to take a closer look at life during that time period. Teams can choose from the following topics to make presentations: Fads, Ingenious Inventions, Sports Figures, Toys and Games, Family Pastimes, Hit Parade of Songs and Dances, Fashion Favorites, Social Etiquette, Celebrated Celebrities, and Hot American Political Topics. Encourage students to find pictures or draw original ones to accompany their presentations.

This Is Your Life, Thomas Dennis Fitzgerald!

It is now 25 years later, and a testimonial dinner is being planned to honor The Great Brain. As part of the celebration, T. D.'s boyhood friends and family have been asked to pay tribute to him. Have each student pretend to be one of the characters from the book and prepare a two-minute presentation. In the speech, each character should expound on how T. D. changed his or her life. Also have each student (from his character's point of view) share an interesting anecdote about The Great Brain.

Game Plans

Children of the 1890s played a variety of games. In chapter 8, the author describes how Tom, J. D., and their friends played Kick The Can. Have students use their imaginations to write directions that explain how to play other games mentioned in the book. Students can select from Heavy, Heavy Hangs Over My Poor Head; Button, Button, Who Has The Button?; Hide The Thimble; or One-O-Cat Ball.

TRAVELING EMPORIUM

Store On Wheels

In chapter 4 the reader meets Abie Glassman, owner of The Traveling Emporium. Reread the description of Abie's wagon in the first pages of the chapter. Discuss with the class the types of merchandise they think Abie sold in 1896. Brainstorm the variety of merchandise that a traveling emporium would carry and sell in the 1990s.

Timeless Dilemmas

The characters in the book faced social issues in the 1890s that are still in the news today. Suicide, religious tolerance, the handicapped, and immigrants and their cultures are all issues interwoven into the story. Have students bring in news-magazine and newspaper articles that deal with these issues. Compare and contrast how these themes were dealt with by various characters in the book and how they are confronted in society today.

The Great Brain's Roots

The author based his book on some of the adventures he had as a child with this older brother, Tom. John D. Fitzgerald grew up to try different occupations, ranging from jazz drummer to newpaper reporter. Make available some of the other books in The Great Brain series (*More Adventures Of The Great Brain, Me And My Little Brain, The Great Brain At The Academy, The Great Brain Reforms, The Return Of The Great Brain,* and *The Great Brain Does It Again*). After students have had opportunities to read some of the further adventures of T. D., have them see if they can find events in the stories that may have influenced the author's adventures as an adult.

About The Author

Share the following information about John D. Fitzgerald with your students:

- John Dennis Fitzgerald was born in 1907 in Utah.
- *The Great Brain* was based on actual experiences the author had with his brother, Tom, as a boy.
- After his father died, Fitzgerald's mother sold the family newspaper. The author got a job with the new owner.
- He spent four years abroad as a foreign correspondent.
- Fitzgerald performed as a jazz drummer.
- The author began to submit stories to magazines and had more than 300 published before 1950.

Penny Candy

Sweeten up your word power! Use the words in the jar to complete the vocabulary contract. Color each piece of candy as you do its activity. Do _____ activities by _____.

_____ (date)

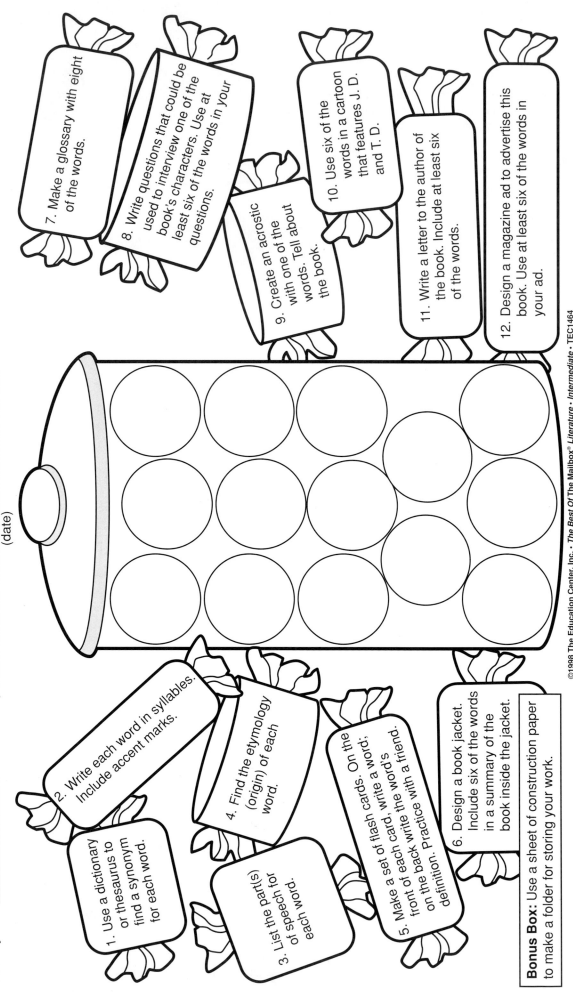

1. Use a dictionary or thesaurus to find a synonym for each word.

2. Write each word in syllables. Include accent marks.

3. List the part(s) of speech for each word.

4. Find the etymology (origin) of each word.

5. Make a set of flash cards. On the front of each card, write a word; on the back write the word's definition. Practice with a friend.

6. Design a book jacket. Include six of the words in a summary of the book inside the jacket.

7. Make a glossary with eight of the words.

8. Write questions that could be used to interview one of the book's characters. Use at least six of the words in your questions.

9. Create an acrostic with one of the words. Tell about the book.

10. Use six of the words in a cartoon that features J. D. and T. D.

11. Write a letter to the author of the book. Include at least six of the words.

12. Design a magazine ad to advertise this book. Use at least six of the words in your ad.

Bonus Box: Use a sheet of construction paper to make a folder for storing your work.

©1998 The Education Center, Inc. • *The Best Of The Mailbox® Literature • Intermediate •* TEC1464

Note To The Teacher: Program the pieces of candy in the candy jar with vocabulary words from *The Great Brain.* (Change the character names in item 10 and use this worksheet with any book in your literature progam.)

Plot Twist Predictions

Oh, how J. D. wished he could outwit and outscheme his brother! Now's the time to come to his rescue by giving the plot new twists. Predict what might have happened to the story line with each of the following changes. Write your predictions on the back of this sheet.

1. T. D. tells his father that Mr. Standish paddled him.

2. J. D. is the Fitzgerald son with all the money "smarts."

3. Before Abie becomes ill, T. D. informs his parents that Abie's strongbox is empty.

4. J. D. advises T. D. to reform, and T. D. gives him the silent treatment.

5. Mr. Fitzgerald is a famous inventor.

6. Sammy Leeds is bullied by Basil.

Bonus Box: Create a plot twist of your own. Ask a friend to relate two changes in the story that would have happened as a result of your plot twist.

Writing Activity Cards: *The Great Brain*

After reading chapters 1 and 2
An often-used punishment at the Fitzgerald house was "the silent treatment." Compose a letter to the editor from The Great Brain telling why parents should *not* use the silent treatment when punishing their children.

After reading chapter 3
J. D.'s older brothers used an unusual method to teach him how to swim. Write about a time in your life when someone taught you how to do something new. Include how you felt before and after you mastered the new skill.

After reading chapter 5
Tom befriends Basil Kokovinis, the Greek immigrant. Tom stated, "I'll make a hundred percent American kid out of him." Make a list of ten things you think a kid needs to have, or be able to do, in order to be 100% American. Illustrate your list.

After reading chapter 6
The Fitzgerald family friend, Abie Glassman, is discovered unconscious in the back of his store. After being carried to the Fitzgerald home, he dies in Mamma's arms. Write a eulogy for Abie's funeral telling his good qualities and why the town will miss him.

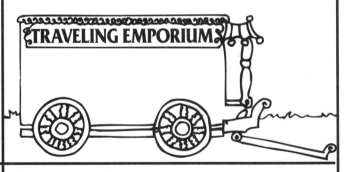

TRAVELING EMPORIUM

After reading chapter 7
The Great Brain devised a plan to get rid of the new teacher, Mr. Standish. All the participants in the plan took an oath to keep it a secret. Later, after the plan succeeded, J. D. blurted out the truth in front of his parents. Write your opinion on whether or not J. D. did the right thing.

After reading chapter 8
The week before Christmas, a miracle took place—The Great Brain's reformation. Imagine that you are Tom. Write a diary entry telling why you acted as you did at the end of the story.

©1998 The Education Center, Inc. • *The Best Of* The Mailbox® *Literature* • *Intermediate* • TEC1464

Note To The Teacher: Glue this page to tagboard and laminate. Cut cards apart. Display on a bulletin board or place at a center. Or give each student a copy of the sheet. The student colors the illustration on each card he completes.

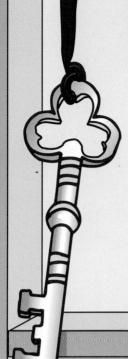

THE INDIAN IN THE CUPBOARD

A Read-Aloud Favorite by
Lynne Reid Banks

Imagine having the power to make toys come alive! For Omri, such an adventure begins when he receives a birthday present that he doesn't even want: a secondhand plastic Indian. With a magical key and a discarded medicine cupboard, Omri embarks on an almost-unbelievable fantasy. Include the following creative teaching ideas and reproducibles with your reading of this wonderful novel.

by Mary Anne Haffner and Sue Ireland

Magic Keys

Build student anticipation and excitement before you begin this adventure. Ask each student to bring a key from home, one that is "retired" or no longer used. If a key is unavailable, a student can create one from gold-colored construction paper. Supply each student with a length of red ribbon so that the key may be worn around his neck. Then announce to the class that in a few days, their keys will unlock *The Indian In The Cupboard.* Ask students to predict what this book might be about.

While enjoying the novel together, remind students that their magical keys will help them to unlock the story's plot. At the conclusion of each chapter, have students identify its key vocabulary words and events. Challenge students to compose their own key questions about the plot so that they can check their comprehension skills.

Unlocking Your Thoughts

Allow students to unlock their critical-thinking skills with these journal-writing topics:

- Omri told Patrick about Little Bear. To whom would *you* tell such a secret? What qualities make this person an excellent choice for sharing such a secret?
- Tommy, a World War I medical orderly, was in a life-threatening situation. Would you send him back into the dangers of war? Explain.
- When he is sent to Mr. Johnson's office, Omri is determined that Patrick will not tell about Little Bear and Boone. How would you have handled this situation if you were Omri?
- You are Omri's parent. You notice that he spends a lot of time in his bedroom and acts strange. What do you say to Omri to find out what is going on?
- You must think of a safe place to hide Little Bear, Boone, and Bright Stars while you go to school. Describe this place.
- Does Omri remind you of yourself? Explain.

A Change Of Heart

Throughout the story, Omri's feelings about Little Bear, Boone, and Bright Stars change. At first, Omri marvels at having the magic to change plastic figures into miniature human beings. Then he realizes that he must play the role of caretaker for his little vulnerable friends.

As you and your class read each chapter, chart how this character development takes place. Divide a sheet of chart paper in half. Label one column "Cause" (what happens to change these feelings) and a second column "Effect" (what change occurred in Omri). After completing the novel, ask students to write paragraphs summarizing the changes that take place in Omri.

What's A *Stereotype?*

Omri based his knowledge of cowboys and Indians on movies and television programs that he had seen. For example, he thought that all Indians lived in tepees. With this type of thinking, he was stereotyping all Native Americans. Discuss with students the meaning of *stereotype* (a fixed view of a group of people). Within cooperative groups, have students look for other examples of times when Omri stereotyped cowboys and Indians. On sentence strips, have each group's recorder list examples of Omri's stereotyping. On the reverse side of each strip, the recorder lists the facts according to Little Bear or Boone. At the end of the session, provide time for each group to share its conclusions with the rest of the class.

Now For The *Real* Facts

Omri decided to find out more about the Iroquois by borrowing *On The Trail Of The Iroquois* from a library. Have your class become experts on the real Iroquois people and the cowboys of the Wild West. Divide students into groups of three or four. Each group chooses a topic to research (see the list below). Have the groups present their findings in booklet form, along with illustrations. Provide time for groups to share their booklets with the class.

TOPICS:
Iroquois: the longhouse, clothing, religion and religious ceremonies, family life and customs, tools and weapons
Cowboys: clothing, horses and saddles, roundups and cattle branding, songs and ballads, the artwork of Charles Russell and Frederic Remington

Blood Brothers And A Truce

Little Bear and Boone try to solve their differences by fighting. It is not until the end of the story that they become blood brothers. They could have settled their differences through *conflict resolution,* a type of truce.

Take your class through this problem-solving process. Divide students into pairs. One partner takes the role of Little Bear, while the other takes the role of Boone. Copy the questions below onto a chart. Have each pair discuss the questions from the characters' perspectives.
- What is the problem?
- Which of your actions contributed to the problem?
- What would you like to see change?
- What three things can you do to achieve this change?
- What would you like the other person to do?
- What will you do and say the next time that this problem arises?

Upon completion of the discussion, have each student write a brief paragraph telling what he or she gained from this activity. Be sure to post the chart in your classroom. When a conflict arises between two students, suggest that they use conflict resolution to settle their differences.

The Adventure Continues

When the novel ends, there is a hint that more adventures may come. What will happen to Little Bear, Boone, Bright Stars, and Tommy? What new plastic figures will come to life? Continue the fantasy with these sequels:
- *The Return Of The Indian:* One year later, Omri and Patrick bring their friends back to life. How will they fight to protect Little Bear's people?
- *The Secret Of The Indian:* Patrick travels back in time to the days of the Wild West. Only this time, he is a miniature version of himself! How can he explain this to a saloon girl and a preacher–turned–piano player?

Your Opinion, Please!

Omri, Patrick, and the other characters in the story were faced with many challenges. Do you think they always made the correct choices? Were there any decisions with which you disagreed? Give your opinion about each situation below.

Directions: Read each sentence. Color the key according to the code.

CODE	
purple = strongly agree	**yellow** = disagree
blue = agree	**red** = strongly disagree

1. Omri should have told his parents about the magic cupboard.

2. Little Bear's scalpings were no worse than acts of terrorism that are committed in the world today.

3. Omri would have remained Patrick's friend even if Omri hadn't told him the secret.

4. Little Bear would make an excellent Iroquois chief.

5. It was more dangerous to leave Little Bear and Boone at home than it was to take them to school.

6. Patrick had no other choice than to confess about Little Bear to the headmaster.

7. It was okay for Omri to sneak some of his parents' whiskey for Boone because the cowboy was used to drinking it.

8. Grown-ups usually know what to do in every situation.

9. Patrick was a better friend to Omri than Omri was to Patrick.

10. Prejudice can be unlearned.

11. Sending Little Bear, Bright Stars, and Boone back into the cupboard was the right decision for Omri to make.

12. *The Indian In The Cupboard* is a book that boys would enjoy more than girls.

Bonus Box: Choose one statement that you strongly agreed with and write three reasons for your opinion. Find a classmate who has the opposite viewpoint. Write his or her three reasons for disagreeing. Compare these opposing viewpoints.

Friends Forever

Little Bear, Boone, and Omri became blood brothers. Each one had special qualities that made this friendship strong.

Directions: For each character, give evidence from the book that supports each trait listed below. Then color the characters and cut on the bold line. Fold on the dotted lines to make a standing display.

Responsibility: _____

Sense of Humor : _____

Courage: _____

Forgiveness: _____

Intelligence: _____

Loyalty: _____

Name _____

In His Wildest Dreams

Each time Omri puts a figure in the cupboard and turns the key, a new and exciting adventure begins. What might have happened if Omri had chosen different plastic miniatures from his collection?

Suppose that each miniature in the cupboard below had entered the story. How would the plot have changed? Use the back of this page to write your answers.

1. Instead of the old Indian chief, Omri puts a modern-day doctor in the cupboard.

2. A horse thief appears when Little Bear is riding in the backyard.

3. Instead of a horse for Little Bear, Omri brings a buffalo to life by mistake.

4. After Little Bear shoots Boone, a western sheriff is brought to life.

5. A judge appears to decide who should care for Boone and Little Bear.

Bonus Box: You can become a part of the adventure! Where and when would you like to show up? Explain on the back of this sheet. Draw yourself in the space below.

Strider

by Beverly Cleary

Fourteen-year-old Leigh Botts's life is pretty ordinary—until Strider, a forlorn, friendless dog, comes on the scene. If your students enjoyed the Newbery award–winning *Dear Mr. Henshaw,* they'll love the further adventures of Leigh Botts in *Strider,* Beverly Cleary's sequel. Extend the reading of this delightful book with the following creative teaching activities and reproducibles.

ideas by Chris Christensen and Irving P. Crump

Mad Minutes

Diaries are very personal records in which people express themselves freely. Most intermediate-age students, however, are apprehensive about sharing their feelings—verbally or in writing. Give your students the opportunity to share—in a fun, nonthreatening manner—their personal feelings about situations paralleling those in *Strider.* First list the following topics on a chalkboard:

- Your room's a total mess. To clean or not to clean: that is the question!
- Which is better—being an only child or having five siblings?
- You have found an abandoned dog. What do you do?
- What do you think about having joint custody of a pet?
- Mr. President often spoke of wanting to make a few changes in this country. What changes would *you* like to make in this country?
- It's important to wear new clothes to show off on the first day of school.
- It's important to wear old clothes on the first day of school—to show that you think school is unimportant.
- Dogs are truly the most noble of animals.

Next have a student select a topic and speak about it before the class for exactly one "mad minute" without stopping (except to breathe!). Tell students that if they run out of things to say, they should not stop, but should continue by using one idea to build upon another. The goal is for each student to express his opinions while staying on the selected topic. For a journal-writing activity, post one of the topics above on the board; then set a kitchen timer for three minutes. Challenge students to write on the topic until the timer goes off.

Even A Tiny Picture Can Be Worth A Thousand Words

During July, Leigh had Strider all to himself, while Barry visited his mom. These were emotional times for Leigh. Use July's diary entries as the basis for a lesson on main-idea development. Provide each student with a large index card. Then direct students to follow these steps:

1. Fold the card in half lengthwise; then reopen it.
2. Cut a pair of 1 1/4-inch slits, two inches apart, in the top half of the card (as shown).
3. Draw and color a simple beach scene between each slit and the edge of the card.
4. Staple seven 2" x 6" strips of paper to the bottom half of the card as shown. On each strip, write the date of a July diary entry and the main idea of that entry.
5. Divide a 1" x 18" strip of white paper into seven, evenly spaced, two-inch-wide frames. Date the frames (in small print at the top righthand corner) in order, to match the seven stapled strips.
6. In each frame, draw and color an illustration to match the main idea on a strip.

When completed, have each student exchange his completed project with a partner. Instruct students to gently pull the illustration strip through the slits to view the pictures and read the matching main ideas.

July 8
Leigh has Strider for the month of July.

Coming To Grips With Conflict

Several diary entries for August and September reveal conflict in the lives of Leigh and those close to him. Discuss with students some of these situations, such as the August 19th entry in which Leigh expresses guilt over not having been nicer to his dad. Next divide your class into five cooperative groups, and assign each group two entries from August through September. Instruct each group to critically evaluate the conflicts, using the following outline as a guide:

- Describe the conflict situation.
- List the events that led up to the conflict.
- Describe how the conflict could have been avoided.
- Describe how the story might have changed if the conflict had not occurred.
- Describe how the conflict was resolved.

After students have had time to analyze the situations, hold a "conflict resolution forum" in which each group shares its findings.

Pam Crane

Pacific Grove Yearbook

Strider is filled with a menagerie of colorful and realistic characters to whom intermediate readers can easily relate. Instruct students to take an even closer look at these characters as they create pages for a "Pacific Grove Yearbook." Provide each student with a 9" x 12" sheet of white construction paper. Instruct each child to draw six boxes on the sheet as shown, leaving space below each box for a character's name and a brief biographical sketch.

Next have each student choose six characters from the book (select from Leigh, Mrs. Botts, Barry, Strider, Mr. Botts, Mr. President, Katy, Bandit, Mrs. Smerling, Kevin, Geneva, Mr. Kurtz) and illustrate each one in a box. Below each character's illustration, instruct the student to add biographical information about the character, list adjectives that describe the character, and briefly explain the character's role in the book. Post the completed pages on a bulletin board entitled "Pacific Grove Yearbook."

Something's Missing!

Leigh began November 25th's entry with "October and November were so boring I didn't have anything to write in my diary." Surely things must have occurred during these two months! But because he felt really "down," Leigh didn't focus on the positive. Have your students reread the entries for October, November, and December.

Next provide each student with a copy of page 74. Have students create diary entries for Leigh using any date during these three months. Draw students' attention to the use of first person when writing diary entries. Also discuss some of the circumstances that may have affected Leigh's mood: the weather was getting colder, the days were getting shorter, and Leigh was confronted with the conflicts discussed in the "Coming To Grips With Conflict" activity on page 72. Mount students' finished writings on a bulletin board entitled "A Day In The Life Of Leigh Botts" or in a class book entitled "The Lost Memoirs Of Leigh Botts."

Problems And Solutions

January, February, and March were a time of problem solving and joy for Leigh. Many diary entries presented problems, while others outlined solutions. Have your students track these situations using the reproducible on page 75. Direct students to complete the chart after reading each diary entry during this time period. Ask students to share ways they may have solved similar problems.

As a follow-up activity, have students share other situations from the book when Leigh could have used some advice. Create a "Dear Blabby" file in which a student identifies a problem, writes about it in a letter format, and signs it "Leigh." Choose a letter to share each day and ask the entire class to write advice-filled responses.

A "New" Shirt

"It was a brand-new shirt my size, a shirt with imagination, a shirt that shouted, 'Buy me! Take me out of here!' " So goes Leigh's description of the colorful shirt that he bought at the thrift shop. On the day before your class is scheduled to read Leigh's July 20th diary entry, invite each student to wear to school his most unusual shirt, T-shirt, or sweater. The next day ask each student to present a monologue to his classmates describing how he obtained the shirt, why he thinks it is so unusual, what the colors or symbols on the shirt represent, and people's reactions to the shirt the first time it was worn.

Dear Diary

During the months of October, November, and December, Leigh wrote very little in his diary. If you were Leigh, what might you have included? Use your creativity to fill in the gaps Leigh left in his diary.

Directions: Reread the few diary entries that Leigh wrote during the months of October, November, and December. Then on the diary pages below, write an entry for a day during those months.

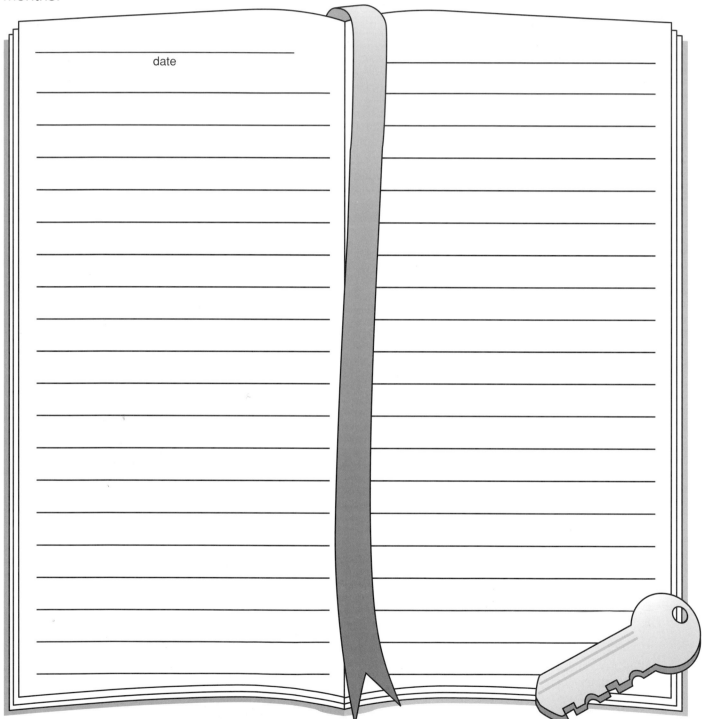

date

Bonus Box: Keep a diary of your own for at least one week. Focus on the positive things that happen each day.

Keeping Track Of Problems

Leigh faced many problems, just like you do! As you read the diary entries from January through the end of March, keep track of the problems Leigh dealt with by logging the information on the chart below. Describe how each problem was handled and how it was finally solved. (Keep in mind that not all of the problems had solutions.) Use the back of this sheet to extend the chart if you need more room.

Keeping Track Of Leigh's Problems

Date	Problem	How problem is handled	Solution

Bonus Box: On the back of this page, write about a recent problem that you have experienced. Describe how you handled the problem. Are you satisfied with the solution to your problem? Explain.

Get A Load Of This!

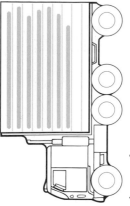

Choose a topic from the list shown and write a paragraph about it on a sheet of notebook paper. After a classmate proofreads your paragraph, copy it onto a lined 4" x 6" index card.

Color the truck and personalize it with your name and your school's name. Cut out the truck along the bold line. Attach the truck to a bulletin board; then "load it" with your rewritten paragraph.

TOPICS

1. Leigh's mom thought that teaching a dog to read was funny. Describe something unusual that you have taught a pet to do.

2. Leigh had mixed feelings about his dad. How do you think divorce affects the children of a family?

3. Do you think it's important to work and earn money for college or to help out with family expenses?

4. Leigh absolutely hated doing the laundry. What chore do you dislike? How could you make the chore a little more pleasant (without having someone else do it!)?

5. On a couple of occasions, Leigh admitted that he "has a bad attitude." Describe a time when you had a bad attitude.

6. Write a paragraph about Strider, but don't include any adjectives or adverbs in your paragraph.

7. By mid-March, Leigh had three friends and was part of the "track crowd." Describe your best friend. Tell about the qualities that make this person your best friend.

8. In his last diary entry, Leigh said that he and Strider had changed since the last summer. How have *you* changed in the past year?

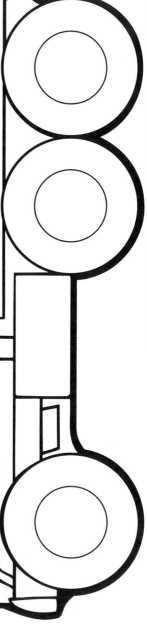

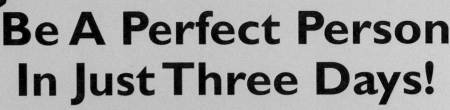

Be A Perfect Person In Just Three Days!

A Read-Aloud Favorite By Stephen Manes

I know what you're thinking! You're thinking, "How can this book possibly teach MY students how to be perfect in just three days?" This humorous, offbeat book about Milo Crinkley's quest for perfection is a must in your plans for celebrating National Humor Month in April. Follow up its reading with these fun activities and reproducibles.

by Jeri L. Nutting

Stand And Deliver

With broccoli dangling around his neck, Milo develops the courage to speak up to the local bully. Give students practice in speaking up to others by having them role-play situations. On large index cards, write the situations listed below. Have two volunteers select a card. Have the pair leave the classroom, practice for a few minutes, and then act out the situation to a satisfactory conclusion before the whole class. To help students get the idea, role-play a situation with another adult.

- Jason, the class bully, keeps knocking your notebook to the floor when he walks by your desk. When you say something to him, he snarls, "Shut up, worm!" Confront Jason.
- Your big sister, Joannie, keeps going into your room and looking through your things. You tell her to stay out, but she ignores you. Confront Joannie.
- Ms. Larson has just given back your math test, and your grade is lower than you expected. When going over the test, you find an item marked incorrect that you're sure is right. Discuss this situation with Ms. Larson.
- Your little brother is continually kicking you while you're both sitting in the backseat of the car. You've had enough, so you kick him back! But Dad sees only what you did and says you'll be punished. Talk to Dad.
- Sally, once your best friend, now puts you down when you're together in a group. She calls you names and talks about you behind your back. Confront Sally.

Perfection Is In The Eye Of The Beholder

Milo thought that he had lots of behaviors that kept him from being "perfect." He fought with his sister, had dumb accidents, played the radio too loudly, and tapped his fingers annoyingly on the table. Ask students to make their own lists of behaviors they would need to get rid of if they were to become "perfect." Have students share their lists; then discuss whether getting rid of those behaviors would make them perfect, or simply better.

Meals That Appeal

Milo had a hard time resisting the temptation to eat his favorite meal, sweet-and-sour wonton. Survey students to find out the foods that they would have the hardest time giving up. Record the data on the chalkboard. Then instruct students to make picture or bar graphs showing the class's favorite foods. Post the graphs in a display area along with magazine pictures of delicious-looking dishes. Extend the lesson further by having students determine what fraction (or percentage) of the foods are fast foods, sweets, carbohydrates, foreign foods, packaged in plastic, or health foods.

Amazing Authors In Just Two Days!

Dr. K. Pinkerton Silverfish is a fictional author who's an expert on becoming perfect. Today many authors write books filled with expert advice for self-improvement. Ask each student to assume the identity of a fictional doctor or author. The student then outlines a self-improvement program like Dr. Silverfish's, including a short "bio" of the author and a brief outline of the steps needed to accomplish the goal. After the outline has been completed, instruct each student to use it to write and illustrate a booklet. Label a shelf in the classroom or media center "Self-Improvement" and display the class's writings. Suggest the following topics, or have students create their own.

- Be A Nintendo Champion In Just…
- Be A Straight-A Student In Just…
- A Crash Course On Being A Chess Champion
- How To Be An Olympic Champion Overnight
- Improve Your Athletic Ability In Just…
- You Can Be Your Parents' Favorite Child In Just…
- Increase Your Intelligence Overnight
- Be The Teacher's Pet In Just…
- How To Be Popular In Just…

The Better To Hear You With, My Dear

When Milo closed his eyes and concentrated on doing nothing, he became very aware of the noises around him. He could sort the car noises from motorcycles or trucks. He heard his stomach churning and gurgling. He heard the TV downstairs and the sounds of people moving around. Teach sensory perception while giving students a change of scenery by taking them on a field trip around the school. Ask students to take notebooks and pencils along. Find a place where your whole group can gather unobtrusively (well, as much as possible!), and sit quietly on the floor or ground. Ask students to close their eyes and listen carefully for a while, then write down what they hear. Share observations. Ask if more is heard with the eyes closed or open. Discuss reasons why.

Presenting The Main Event

What were the highlights of the story? To find out what the students think, divide them into groups of four to six each. Ask each group to make a list of the main events in the story and to give reasons for their choices. After a sharing time by each group, have each student in the class draw a five-panel cartoon showing his or her selections of the main events. The cartoons should include characters along with dialogue. Provide crayons or colored pencils so that the cartoons can be "colorized." Combine all the cartoons into a booklet entitled *Manes's Main Events*.

Jeri Nutting taught grades two to six for 20 years in Atlanta, Tampa, and Orlando. Currently living in Greensboro, North Carolina, she is a free-lance writer and does volunteer work in local schools.

Are You A Storyteller?

Creative thinking/writing

Milo made up stories to explain why he was wearing a stalk of broccoli around his neck. How quickly could you think on your feet if you found yourself in such an unusual situation?

Read each question below. Use your creativity to write a believable explanation to give your parents, friends, or teachers. Be original and convincing like Milo! Use the back of this sheet if you need more space.

What would you say if people asked why...

1. you came to school one day dressed in red from head to toe?_____

_____

_____

2. you didn't talk at all for a whole day? _____

_____

_____

3. you carried a head of lettuce under your arm all day?_____

_____

_____

4. you began with, "That's all right, Sam," each time you spoke to someone?_____

_____

_____

5. you wore your clothes inside out for an entire day? _____

_____

_____

6. you kept a smelly clove of garlic in your pocket all day? _____

_____

_____

7. you wore a glove on your left hand all day? _____

_____

_____

Bonus Box: Choose one of the situations above. Write a story telling about the reasons for your behavior and the result. Include people's reactions to your reasons.

It Always Rains In Maine!

Every year when you visit Aunt Hildegard in Portland, Maine, it rains. When you complain, "It rains here all the time!," you're making a general statement, or *generalization*, about the weather in Maine. The statement is based on your facts and own experience. Generalizations may be *valid* (true) or *invalid* (not true). Since weather records for Portland show that it rains or snows an average of 127 days a year, your generalization about the weather in Maine is invalid!

Read each paragraph below. On the lines, write a generalization about each character based on the information in the paragraph. Use the back of this sheet if you need more space.

1. The picture showed a man wearing baggy, zebra-striped pants, a shirt with two buttons missing, half of a bow tie, and a bent hat with feathers sticking up from the headband. Dr. Silverfish wore a clown nose and was biting a hot dog, dripping mustard.

   Write a generalization about Dr. Silverfish.

   _____

   _____

   _____

2. Milo told his parents that he was wearing broccoli because he was doing a school play about nutrition. He told his friends he had a terrible disease and the broccoli would cure him. He told his teachers he was wearing it because of his doctor's orders.

   Write a generalization about Milo.

   _____

   _____

   _____

3. Mr. Crinkley was concerned because Milo wasn't eating his meals. He read Milo's book and did not insist that Milo eat. On Day 3, Mr. Crinkley brought him some weak tea. He also made a "Do Not Disturb" sign for Milo's door and told the family not to bother Milo.

   Write a generalization about Mr. Crinkley.

   _____

   _____

   _____

4. Dr. Silverfish gave strict instructions on being perfect. When Milo doubted his wisdom, Dr. Silverfish's picture glowered at Milo. Dr. Silverfish taught Milo about willpower and completing jobs. Sometimes Dr. Silverfish cracked jokes in his book. When Milo finished the book, Dr. Silverfish almost seemed to wink at Milo from the back cover.

   Write a generalization about Dr. Silverfish.

   _____

   _____

   _____

Bonus Box: On the back of this sheet, tell whether each of your generalizations is valid or invalid. Give reasons for your decisions.

Be A Perfect Person In Just Three Days!
Creative-writing contract

Bet Your Broccoli You Can Write!

Color each book cover as you finish the assignment.

Be A Really "Rad" Reporter!

Interview Dr. Silverfish about his new book, *Make Four Billion Dollars By Next Thursday!* Write your questions and his responses.

The Perfect People Club

Pretend that Dr. Silverfish included an application for the Perfect People Club in his book. Design and write the application for the club.

Superb Speech Writing

Write a speech about not being perfect and still being happy with yourself. Practice the speech and present it to the class.

Be The Perfect Poet

Write a two-word poem about broccoli. Include as many lines as you want—but use only two words per line! Your poem doesn't have to rhyme.

"Let's see. What rhymes with *broccoli* ?"

A Gourmet's Guide To Great Food

Milo ate weird things like pickles and salami for breakfast. Write menus for breakfast, lunch, and dinner that include all the weird food you enjoy (and that your parents don't usually let you eat!).

Stylish Scripts

Write a script for a radio advertisement for *Be A Perfect Person In Just Three Days!* Gather the props you'll need to make sound effects to use in the ad. Practice and then tape the ad.

My Personal Journal

Milo fought with his sister a lot. Write about a time that you got into an argument with someone in your family. Share what the argument was about and how it was resolved.

Letters To Authors

A short biographical sketch of Stephen Manes is at the end of the book. Describing his life as a writer, Manes says, "It's okay, I guess." Write a pretend letter to the author telling him your feelings about the book. Ask him to explain his statement.

Note To The Teacher: Before duplicating this page, fill in the number of activities and the due date. If you prefer, use any of these as whole-class activities.

In The Year Of The Boar

by Bette Bao Lord

In the Chinese calendar, 1947 is the year of the boar. It's also the year that a black baseball star named Jackie Robinson captures all the hearts of Brooklyn—especially the one belonging to Shirley Temple Wong. Follow up Bette Bao Lord's autobiographical account of a young girl adjusting to a new country with these creative teaching ideas and reproducibles.

by Mary Anne Haffner and Sue Ireland

East Meets West

Bette Bao Lord's book provides an interesting glimpse into Chinese culture. It also reveals some attitudes that sharply contrast with our "American style" of life. Lead a classroom discussion about some of the social customs that Shirley's family brings to America. Challenge students to find examples of customs in the story, then compare and contrast this Oriental way of thinking with what the family finds in their new homeland. Include these examples:

- the role of the wife
- feelings about death and the afterlife
- giving and receiving compliments
- running a household
- signs of affection and gift giving
- the place of the elderly in a family

What's The Lineup?

Explain to students that the beginning of a book usually presents the characters and when and where the action takes place. The middle of the book presents the conflict, or problem, faced by the main character. The ending reveals the solution to the problem. On a large sheet of art paper, have each student draw a baseball diamond as shown. Discuss the components of this "story map"; then direct students to fill in the bases on their papers. Have them fill in the diamonds with illustrations of favorite parts of the book.

2nd base: Conflict?

3rd base: Solution?

1st base: Characters? Setting?

Home Plate: Summary

A Power-Packed Speech

Get your students thinking about the power of the spoken word. Reread Mrs. Rappaport's emotional response to the question "…is there something special about baseball that fits the special kind of people we are and the special kind of country America is?" (found in the chapter "June: I Pledge a Lesson to the Frog"). Allow interested students the opportunity to give dramatic readings of the speech the way they think Shirley's teacher gave it. Discuss with students what makes the speech such a powerful one. Share excerpts from other inspiring speeches such as Abraham Lincoln's Gettysburg Address, John F. Kennedy's inaugural address, and Martin Luther King, Jr.'s "I Have A Dream" speech. Then give students an opportunity to write and present speeches on topics they feel strongly about. Suggest the following titles or encourage students to choose their own:

- America—What Makes Us A Great Country
- People—All Different, All Alike
- Freedom
- Friendship
- Honesty
- The Value Of Education

And Jackie Robinson

Rookies Of The Year

After reading the book, lead students in a discussion of the similarities between Shirley Temple Wong and Jackie Robinson. Use the following quotes as discussion starters:

"Upon your shoulders rests the reputation of all Chinese."
— *Shirley's mother to Shirley*
"…I need more than a great player. I need a man who will accept insults, take abuse…in a word, carry the flag for his race."
— *Branch Rickey, General Manager of the Brooklyn Dodgers, to Jackie Robinson*

Wrap It Up

Turn a class project into a treasured memento to share with other classes. Divide students into 12 groups and assign each group a chapter of the book. Provide each group with two 6" x 6" pieces of tagboard. On one piece of tagboard, the group draws the Chinese character (found on the first page of the chapter), adds the chapter title, and includes a brief summary of the main events. On the second sheet, each group illustrates an important event in the chapter. The two completed pages are pasted back-to-back and laminated. Punch holes in all 12 pages and combine into a booklet with a metal binder ring. Allow each student to take the booklet home to share with his family. Then place the booklet in the media center for a while before making it a permanent part of your classroom library.

一
月
January
Chinese New Year
Bandit's father plans to make America his family's home. Bandit's new name is Shirley Temple Wong.

It's A Homer!

Divide students into all-star cooperative teams to face the following lineup of critical-thinking questions. Photocopy the questions, one copy per team. The teams choose questions from the list that will total a home run (four points). Let groups answer the questions orally or in writing.

Singles (one point)

- Before Bandit left for America, she chose a new name: Shirley Temple Wong. If you were changing names, what famous name would you each choose? Why?
- On Shirley's first day in America, she became lost. What three things would you do if you were lost in a strange neighborhood?
- If you were a classmate of Shirley's at P.S. 8, how would you make her feel welcomed?

Doubles (two points)

- When Shirley was asked to stop playing stoop ball, she stayed and watched "like a hungry ghost." Explain why you think the author used this description. Write two similes of your own, beginning with "Shirley stood watching like…"
- Do you agree or disagree with Shirley's decision not to tell her parents about Mabel and the black eyes? Explain.
- Compare the two teachers in Shirley's life: Mrs. Rappaport and Señora Rodriguez. How did each person help Shirley believe in herself?

Triples (three points)

- Shirley had some real problems when she baby-sat the O'Reilly triplets. Design a plan so that Shirley could tell the three boys apart.
- Which character in the story do you think is Shirley's best friend? Which character in the story do each of you think would be your best friend? Explain.
- Predict what will happen to Shirley as she enters sixth grade. How will her life change after her new brother or sister is born?

A Little Wisdom, Please!

Shirley learned that in America one does not have to be old to be wise. How about you? Do you think you're wise? Read the following problems from the book. Write how you would have solved each one. Use the back of this sheet if you need more room.

1. Shirley didn't know English when she moved to America.
    _____
    _____

2. The Wong family wanted to be both Chinese and American.
    _____
    _____

3. Shirley was not looking forward to a lonely summer. _____
    _____
    _____

4. Shirley was told that she had to be "China's little ambassador." _____
    _____
    _____

5. Mr. and Mrs. Wong wanted the truth about Shirley's black eyes. _____
    _____
    _____

6. The Terrible Threesome would not behave when Shirley was baby-sitting. _____
    _____
    _____

7. Shirley was sad when the Dodgers lost the World Series. _____
    _____
    _____

8. Shirley felt embarrassed about her mistakes. _____
    _____
    _____

9. Taking piano lessons was hard for Shirley. _____
    _____
    _____

10. Shirley needed money for her piggy bank. _____
    _____
    _____

Bonus Box: The Chinese have many wise sayings. Make up a wise saying about solving problems.

The Year Of The Boar And More

What a great year 1947 was for Shirley and her friends! What a great year this is for you! Complete the chart below by comparing 1947 with the present year. Then answer the two questions below the chart.

Category	1947	Now
cartoon characters	Donald Duck Chip and Dale	
baseball stars	Jackie Robinson Joe DiMaggio	
expressions	"Gee whiz!" "Fat chance!"	
popular movie stars	Katharine Hepburn Ronald Colman	
sweet treats	penny candy Juicy Fruit gum	
U.S. president	Harry S. Truman	
family activities	playing board games listening to the radio	
favorite book series	Nancy Drew mysteries Zane Grey westerns	
popular songs	"Zip-A-Dee-Doo-Dah" "Sixteen Tons"	
price of a gallon of milk	78¢	
price of a one-pound loaf of bread	13¢	
ways for kids to earn money	baby-sitting	

How is the present year better than 1947? _____

_____

What things of 1947 would you like to see today? _____

_____

Bonus Box: On the back of this page, list five more categories for the chart. List items for the present year; then research to find items for 1947.

It's Your Year!

The Chinese name each year after an animal. Find the year you were born and color the box yellow. Then follow the directions below. Use the back if you need more space.

1. What part of the description in your box best describes you? Explain. _____
   _____
   _____

2. Think of other qualities that you have. List and describe three that could be added in your box.
   _____
   _____
   _____

3. Shirley was born in 1938, the Year of the Tiger. What qualities in her box best describe her? Explain.
   _____
   _____
   _____

4. List and describe three personality traits of Shirley's father. _____
   _____
   _____
   _____

5. List and describe three personality traits of Shirley's mother. _____
   _____
   _____

6. What kind of teacher do you think Mrs. Rappaport was? Find and list three examples from the book that support your opinion. _____
   _____
   _____

Bonus Box: Research to find the other six animals that the Chinese use in their calendar.

Year of the Tiger
1938, 1950, 1962, 1974, 1986, 1998
People born this year have a great sense of humor. They are brave and make natural leaders.

Year of the Rabbit
1939, 1951, 1963, 1975, 1987, 1999
People born this year are kind, gracious, and friendly. They are popular, but they are modest. They are also very lucky.

Year of the Dragon
1940, 1952, 1964, 1976, 1988, 2000
People born this year are outgoing. They are strong and full of energy. They are deep thinkers and have vivid imaginations.

Year of the Snake
1941, 1953, 1965, 1977, 1989, 2001
People born this year are wise and talented. They are intuitive. They are good at making money and like nice things.

Year of the Horse
1942, 1954, 1966, 1978, 1990, 2002
People born this year are confident, optimistic, and energetic. They make friends easily, but they like to travel alone.

The True Confessions Of Charlotte Doyle

A Newbery Honor Book
by Avi

Travel back in time to the summer of 1832. Step onto the deck of the *Seahawk* and join 13-year-old Charlotte Doyle, a ruthless captain, and a mutinous crew in a spellbinding tale of murder on the high seas. Enhance the reading of this award-winning historical fiction novel with the following creative teaching suggestions and reproducibles.

by Mary Anne Haffner

Booking Passage On The *Seahawk*

Pique student interest in this novel with a prereading activity. Use assorted art materials to turn a tan cardboard box into a traveling trunk (or bring a real one from home). Label the trunk "Charlotte Doyle, Benevolent Street, Providence, Rhode Island." Inside the trunk, place copies of the book; a world map with a Liverpool, England–to–Providence, Rhode Island, sea route drawn on it; a chess set; a teapot; a round robin (see chapter 5 in the book); a lock of hair tied with ribbon; a key; and a blank journal*.

Share each item in the trunk with your class; then read aloud the book's prologue ("An Important Warning"). Ask students what they now know about Charlotte and what they want to know about her. Elicit further predictions about the novel. Ask a volunteer to record these ideas in the blank journal. Then tell students to get set for the adventure of a lifetime!

The journal is needed to complete the culminating activity on page 88, "Your Journey Ends." Store it in the trunk as a souvenir of your travels.

A Little Research, Please

In writing historical fiction, an author must research certain aspects of the time period in which his story takes place. What did Avi need to know before writing Charlotte's story? Send teams of researchers armed with notecards to the media center to dive into the following topics:

- How did upper-class English and American ladies dress during the early 19th century?
- What rules of behavior dictated the day-to-day lives of 19th-century women?
- The *Seahawk* was a brig. What working vocabulary did sailors need to do their jobs? (See the appendix at the back of the book.)
- What kinds of tools and knot-making techniques were used by sailors?
- What must the captain of any sailing vessel know about wind currents and weather?
- After reading "Ship's Time" in the book's appendix, explain this system to the class.

After completing their notes, have students rewrite their information onto copies of the brig pattern on page 90. Have students cut out their brigs; then attach the cutouts to a bulletin board entitled "High-Seas Research."

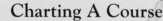

Charting A Course

Challenge students to explore the many elements of this exciting book's structure, plot, and characterization. Divide your class into discussion crews of four students each. For each crew, duplicate pages 89–90, which provide job descriptions for each crew, guidelines for successful cooperative learning, and discussion questions for each chapter in the book. Provide each crew with chart paper and markers, plus an envelope for storing the discussion cards. Instruct each admiral to remove and discuss only the cards for chapters that have been read. Display each crew's chart on a magnetic chalkboard or a bulletin board for easy reference.

Charlotte's Journal

Charlotte's father gave her a journal to record the events of the voyage. Turn this idea into a journal experience for your own students. After students complete an assigned reading, have each one make an SOS entry: *S* for *Summary* of events, *O* for *Opinions* or *Observations* about the plot, and *S* for *Sketch*. Students should limit their summaries and opinions/observations to two sentences each. For sketches, have students draw simple objects or symbols. Add these journals to your students' language arts portfolios.

Drama On The High Seas

Enhance your students' enjoyment of Charlotte's suspenseful adventure with dramatic readings. Ask volunteers to present Charlotte's trial in chapter 18, assuming the roles of Charlotte, Captain Jaggery, and the other characters. (Costumes and props aren't necessary, but would add a more realistic touch.) Since the book is a first-person account, have students include Charlotte's inner thoughts and descriptions of the trial in the dramatization. While Charlotte reads the narration, have the other actors turn their backs to the audience. This will help the audience distinguish between narration and actual dialogue. Videotape the presentation if possible. Get set for some Academy Award–winning performances! *(Chapters 19 and 21, as well as the end of chapter 22, are additional sections suitable for dramatization.)*

A Quote Quilt

Enlist your crew's artistic talents to create a quote quilt. Assign each pair of students one character: Charlotte, Mr. Grummage, Captain Jaggery, Keetch, Barlow, Mr. Hollybrass, Zachariah, Fisk, Cranick, Ewing, Morgan, Foley, Dillingham, Grimes, Mr. Doyle, Mrs. Doyle, Evelina, Albert, Bridget, or Mary. Instruct each pair to locate a description of the character or a direct quote made by him or her. Provide each pair with an eight-inch, white paper square. Have the students include the character's name, an illustration, and the description/quote in the design of the square. Mount each square on a nine-inch construction-paper square. For durability, laminate the completed squares. Ask volunteers to arrange the squares to make a quilt; then bind the squares together with masking tape on the back. *(Two helpful hints: Have students use calligraphy or fine-line markers to letter their quotes. A script style of writing would be authentic for the early 1800s. Include a square in the center of the quilt featuring the book's title and author. Include some quotes from the book jacket on this square.)*

Your Journey Ends

As a culminating activity, ask each student to write a brief entry for the blank journal in Charlotte's trunk. Have each student write his entry on a small index card; then paste each card onto a journal page. Suggest these topics to your students:

- Tell how reading the book has changed you— as a reader and a writer.
- Explain why you think the novel was chosen as a Newbery Honor Book in 1991.
- Write an invitation to read the novel to another class in your school. Use a suspenseful tone without revealing any major plots.
- Describe the book and its plot in a ten-word list. Include five adjectives and five action verbs.
- Write a paragraph that might have appeared in the captain's log. For a mysterious touch, tear the paragraph in half so that the reader has only half of the entry.

Be sure to include your own entry in the journal! Place the completed journal in the trunk; then pass the trunk on to another class in your school. Inform those students that you found the trunk in the attic of an old, deserted house, and you just don't know what to make of it....

Charting A Course

Ready to set off on your adventure with Charlotte on the *Seahawk?* The following guidelines will help your crew stay on course!

Crew Members' Job Descriptions
The **Admiral** reads the questions and makes sure that every member responds to each one.
The **Log Keeper** makes notes of important points made by the crew.
The **First Mate** lists on a chart one important point made by each crew member.
The **Captain** reports the high points of the discussion to the class.

Rules Of The Sea
1. Speak softly.
2. Speak one at a time.
3. Value others' opinions.
4. Stay on task.
5. Rotate jobs so that crew members experience each role.
6. Cite evidence from the book to support your views.

Chapter 1

What did you learn about Charlotte's education and social class? *Foreshadowing* is a technique writers use to warn the reader of what lies ahead. What events and descriptions give this chapter a mysterious tone?

Chapter 2

How is a mood of suspense built into this chapter? How does each character add to the suspense? If you were Charlotte, what conditions on the ship would you find appalling? Would you want to get off the ship? Why or why not?

Chapter 3

Cite evidence of Charlotte's feelings for Captain Jaggery and for the crew. If Charlotte asked for your observations of the men, what would you say?

Chapter 4

Should Charlotte trust Zachariah? Would you keep the dirk? A *naive* person is one who does not have the experience to truly understand a situation. Which of Charlotte's ideas prove she is naive?

Chapter 5

Use five adjectives to describe Captain Jaggery. What leadership qualities does he have? Would you trust him? Why or why not?

Chapter 6

Charlotte said, "I felt like a princess...." How would you respond to her? How would you feel being all alone in the cargo area?

Chapter 7

Why is Charlotte being courted for her friendship? "...too many puzzles. Too many complexities." What parts of the plot puzzle you?

Chapter 8

Whom would you befriend—Captain Jaggery or Zachariah? On what conclusions would you base your friendship?

Chapter 9

Would you tell the captain what you have seen and heard? What situations call for safety first, rather than friendship?

Chapter 10

Why did the author make Cranick the stowaway? Divide your crew into two sides. Have one side justify the captain's actions; have the other condemn them.

Chapter 11

Pretend you're the captain. Comment on Charlotte's behavior. Pretend you are Charlotte and have been left alone. What will you do now?

Chapter 12

How has Charlotte changed—physically and mentally—up to this part of the book?

Note To The Teacher: See "Charting A Course" on page 87 for information on how to use the discussion cards on this page and the top half of page 90.

Pattern
Use with "A Little Research, Please" on page 87.

Chapter 14

"He's waiting, wanting you to make a mistake...." If you were a crew member, why would you agree with this statement? What evidence supports your predictions for the rest of the novel?

Chapter 16

Accused of murder! What evidence makes Charlotte appear guilty? Innocent? Pretend you're Zachariah. What will you tell Charlotte?

Chapter 18

What evidence would you offer in Charlotte's defense? Does the trial seem believable to you? Why or why not?

Chapter 20

"This book is a real page-turner!" What does this expression mean? Two more chapters to go—what has you on the edge of your seat?

Chapter 22

Give your impressions of Charlotte's family. If you were Charlotte, would you share your journal with your father? What clues did the author give that the novel would end this way? Will Charlotte ever return to her parents' home?

Chapter 13

Why did the author have Charlotte meet a physical challenge to prove herself to the crew? Reread the last sentence of this chapter. Why did the author choose to end it this way?

Chapter 15

What does the hurricane symbolize? What mood is created in this chapter? Zachariah—is he a ghost or real?

Chapter 17

Why do you empathize with Charlotte and Zachariah? Why does the author want to bring out these feelings in you, the reader?

Chapter 19

How would you reassure Charlotte that Zachariah is on her side? How would you get the captain to confess to murder?

Chapter 21

Pretend you're a crew member. Why are you relieved that the captain is dead and Charlotte is now in command?

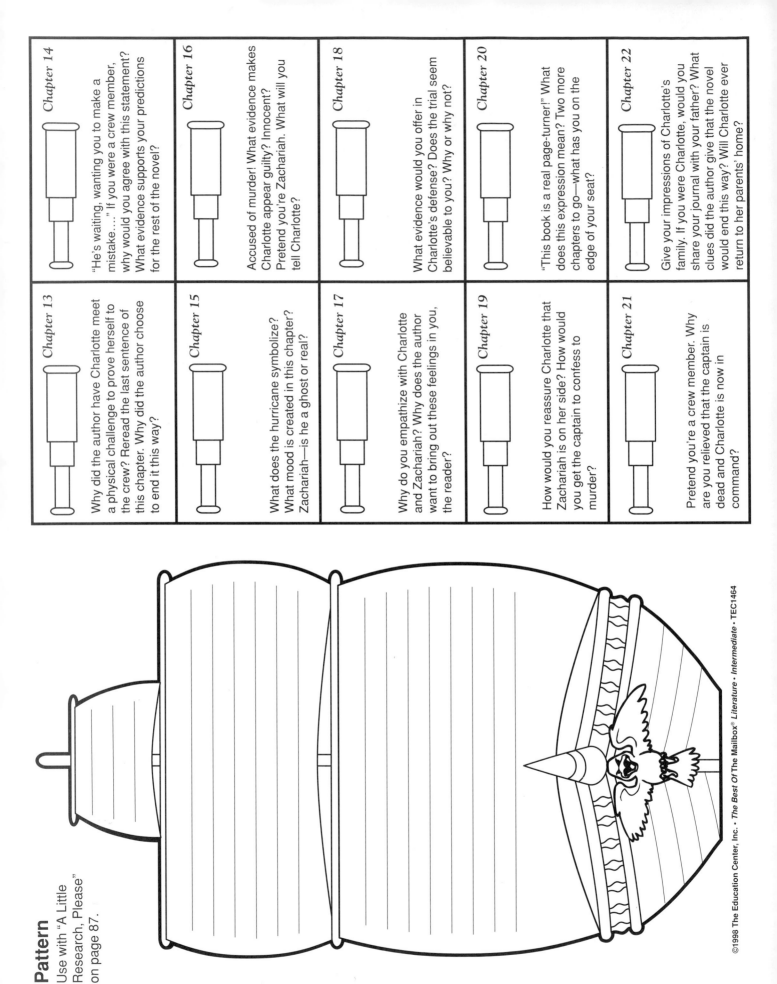

A Twist Of Fate

Avi, the author of *The True Confessions Of Charlotte Doyle*, filled his novel with loads of suspense and exciting plot twists.

Pretend that you are the author. Cut out the ten boxes below. Paste each box to the top of a 4" x 6" index card. Below each box, complete the "If...then" statement with a picture. Then—below the picture—describe your illustration.

1 If the other passengers had shown up to make the voyage, then…

2 If Charlotte had given the dirk to the captain, then…

3 If Charlotte had prevented Zachariah from being beaten, then…

4 If Charlotte had been sentenced to die one hour after her trial, then…

5 If the crew had rejected Charlotte's friendship, then…

6 If Captain Jaggery had realized that he had actually seen Zachariah during the hurricane, then…

7 If Charlotte had saved Captain Jaggery from falling overboard, then…

8 If Mr. Doyle had believed the contents of Charlotte's journal, then…

9 If Charlotte had decided to remain in Providence with her family, then…

10 If the title of the book were changed to *The True Confessions Of Charles Doyle,* then…

Bonus Box: Punch a hole in the top left-hand corner of each index card where shown by the circle. Use a wire tie or book ring to combine your cards into a booklet.

©1998 The Education Center, Inc. • *The Best Of* The Mailbox® *Literature* • *Intermediate* • TEC1464

Note To The Teacher: Provide each student with ten 4" x 6" index cards, scissors, and paste or glue.

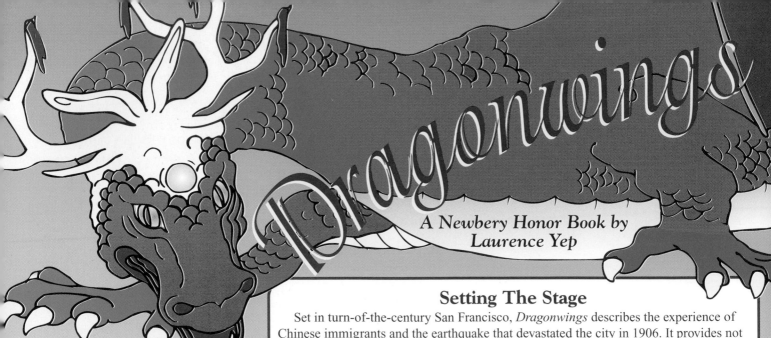

Dragonwings

A Newbery Honor Book by Laurence Yep

It's 1903, and eight-year-old Moon Shadow is leaving his home in China for San Francisco, where he will live with the father he has never known. A sensitive tribute to the Chinese-American experience, *Dragonwings* exquisitely details the challenges Moon Shadow faces as he struggles with a new culture and embraces his father's dream of building a flying machine. Savor this gripping historical novel with students during Aviation History Month in November or anytime your sights are set on an unforgettable reading adventure.

*by Chris Christensen and
Becky Andrews*

Setting The Stage

Set in turn-of-the-century San Francisco, *Dragonwings* describes the experience of Chinese immigrants and the earthquake that devastated the city in 1906. It provides not only don't-miss opportunities to explore a fascinating period in America's history, but it's also the perfect literature complement to a science unit on aviation or earthquakes.

Take advantage of these cross-curricular connections with a prereading research activity. One or two weeks before beginning the book, divide the class into research teams. Give each team one of the topics listed below and these materials: two large, equal-sized pieces of heavy cardboard; clear sealing tape; poster board; scissors; and glue. Have each team tape the cardboard pieces together with clear sealing tape to make a standing display that will fold easily. Next have the team cover one side of its display with poster board. Have students in each team research their assigned topic; then have students decorate their board with facts and illustrations about the topic. After students share with their classmates, have teams place displays around the room for easy reference while reading *Dragonwings.*

Research topics:

1906 San Francisco earthquake	Boxer Rebellion	the Wright Brothers
turn-of-the-century San Francisco	Oriental Exclusion Acts	California Gold Rush
	Central Pacific Railroad	

Old Country, New Country

Laurence Yep artfully describes the Chinese community in San Francisco and its ties to the old country. Before beginning *Dragonwings,* divide a large piece of chart paper into two columns, **Ties To China** and **Adaptations To America.** Explain to students that as they read (or listen to you read), they should look for examples of how some of the characters maintain ties to China while they also adapt to the American culture. List these examples on the chart as students identify them. Ask students who may be first- or second-generation Americans to share ways that their families have incorporated homeland traditions into their lives in America.

Seven Years In 12 Chapters

Laurence Yep chronicles Moon Shadow's first seven years in America in 12 dated chapters. Create a pictorial timeline of Moon Shadow's adventures while reading *Dragonwings.* To begin, label a large, unlined index card with the book's title; then punch two holes in the bottom of the card. Mount the card at the top of a bulletin board or door. After reading the first chapter, write the chapter's date at the top of a large, unlined index card. Punch two holes at the top and at the bottom of the card; then give the card to a small group of students. Have the group decide on the most critical event of the chapter and illustrate it on the card. Students should also add a summarizing caption on the card. Attach the chapter card to the title card using two twist-ties as shown. Continue adding a card after each chapter. To vary, have student pairs or cooperative teams make their own timelines; then compare the finished timelines as an innovative way to review the book.

Dear Mother And Grandmother

When Moon Shadow sails for San Francisco, he leaves behind his mother and grandmother. The two women live for the days when letters arrive from America. As a quick and easy comprehension check after each chapter, have students write letters to Moon Shadow's mother and grandmother. Writing from Moon Shadow's point of view, have students tell about recent happenings in San Francisco, the Company's laundry, and Moon Shadow's new life. It's a great way to hone summarizing skills and check students' understanding of the book's plot, setting, and characters.

The Company

Moon Shadow and his father belong to the Company, a group of men who work and live together at their laundry in Chinatown. With loyalty and a willingness to sacrifice for one another, the Company exemplifies friendship in a way that is rare today. Have students brainstorm examples of loyalty and self-sacrifice demonstrated by members of the Company. List them on the chalkboard; then discuss the following questions: Why do you think the men of the Company were so committed to one another? What do you think of Uncle's leadership of the Company? If you had been a member of the Company, how would you have handled Black Dog? What groups or organizations today remind you in some way of the Company? What qualities of friendship did the Company demonstrate?

After the discussion, create photo-essays on the theme of friendship. Have each student cut pictures that tell a story about friendship from old magazines—friendship between a mother and child, peer to peer, etc. Give each child a piece of art paper on which to glue his pictures. Be sure students add titles to their photo-essays before displaying them on a "Friendship Gallery" bulletin board. Challenge students to interpret the story that each essay is trying to tell.

A Superior Man

Throughout the book, Uncle repeats expressions about "A superior man…." As you read the story, point out these proverbial statements and discuss their interpretations. For fun, list the following proverb starters (or ones of your own) on the board:

- A superior student….
- A superior pet….
- A superior mom/dad….
- A superior school….
- A superior friend….
- A superior vacation….
- A superior teacher….
- A superior video game….

Have each student select a starter from the list, copy it on a strip of paper, and finish it; then have him fold the strip and drop it into a fishbowl or other container. When you find yourself with an extra five minutes of class time, ask a student to draw one of the slips, read it to the class, and lead a brief discussion of the proverb.

Character Conversations

Dragonwings is populated with a rich cast of characters, perfect for characterization investigations. As students read the book, have each child write each main character's name at the top of a blank page in his reading journal. Instruct students to make notes about each character's appearance, important quotes, behavior, attitudes toward America and Windrider's dream—anything that might give someone an understanding of that character. At the end of the book, divide the class into pairs. Instruct each pair to choose two characters and write a conversation they might have. Make sure that the conversation reflects what the students know about the characters. Let students practice reading their conversations and present them to the class.

Simply Superior!

a b c d e f g h i j k l m n o p q r s t u v w x y z

A B C D E F G H I

J K L M N O P Q

R S T U V W X Y Z

Superior men help one another in time of need.
The superior man tends his own garden.
A superior man admits the truth.

Student Directions:
Uncle was known for repeating proverbs that usually began "A superior man…." Some of these proverbs were probably written on the long, narrow strips of red paper that decorated the walls of the Company's laundry. On the lines, try your hand at copying some of Uncle's proverbs using the special alphabet in the box.

_____

_____

_____

_____

_____

_____

_____

_____

_____

_____

_____

_____

_____

On another piece of paper or the back of this sheet, copy and finish the following proverb starters. Try to use the special alphabet.

- A superior pal….
- A superior book….
- A superior neighbor….
- A superior day at school….

Note To The Teacher: Provide each student with a fine-tipped black marker, a 4" x 12" strip of red bulletin-board paper, a new pencil, and a length of yarn. Have the student use a pencil to copy one of his proverbs vertically on the red paper; then have him trace his writing with the black marker. Tape the top of the strip to the pencil. Tie the ends of the yarn to the ends of the pencil to make a hanger. Hang the strips from a bulletin board.

Words About Windrider

If you asked the characters below to give their opinions about Windrider's dream of flying, what would each person say? Use what you learned about each character from reading *Dragonwings* to fill in the blanks with that person's opinion.

Miss Whitlaw	Moon Shadow	Uncle Bright Star
I _____	I _____	I _____

Mother	Robin	Black Dog
I _____	I _____	I _____

Bonus Box: At the end of the book, Moon Shadow said, "I had found my mountain of gold, after all, and it had not been nuggets but people who had made it up." What people have been "nuggets of gold" in your life? List the people on the back of this page. Beside each name, tell why you selected that person to be on your list. Share your list with a friend.

Riding On The Winds Of A Dream!

Windrider once said, "Life is too short to spend it pursuing little things." He had a big dream—to build a flying machine. What BIG dream do you want to pursue? Write about your dream on the kite; then cut out the kite and the pattern. Use the pattern, construction paper, and a piece of yarn to make a kite tail to tape to your kite. Then follow the directions to make a kite that will really fly!

Materials: one sheet of duplicating paper   scissors
pencil   tape
stapler   hole puncher
tongue depressor or Popsicle® stick   string or yarn

Fold; crease on dotted line only.

Punch hole through fold.

Staple.

Directions:

1. Fold the paper in half lengthwise, but DON'T crease the fold.

2. Crease the fold just past the midpoint of the fold. This forms the kite's *keel.*

3. Fold the two top corners to the keel. Staple the corners to the keel about 1 1/2 inches from the top.

4. Mark a dot on the keel just above the midpoint.

5. Put a piece of clear tape over the dot on both sides of the kite to reinforce the paper.

6. Punch a hole through the fold at the dot.

7. Tie one end of the string through the two holes; knot it securely.

8. Tie the other end of the string to the tongue depressor.

9. Find some steady wind and fly!

Name _____

My BIG Dream

Pattern

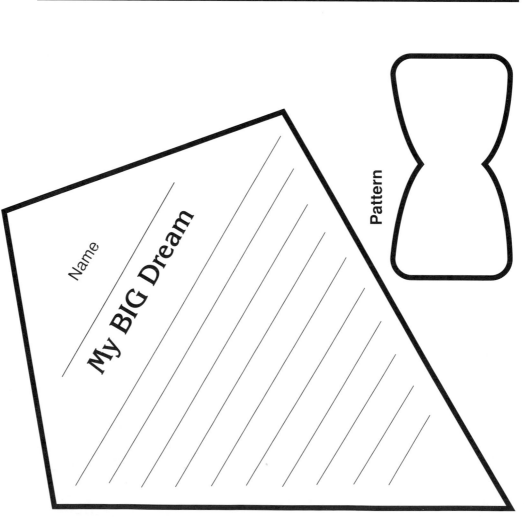

Note To The Teacher: Provide each student with construction paper and the kite-making materials listed in the box. Have the student glue his finished kite cutout (without the tail) to a colorful piece of construction paper; then have him cut around the cutout so that a border of color shows. After students have added kite tails to their cutouts, post the cutouts on a bulletin board titled "Our High-Flying Dreams."

The Best Christmas Pageant Ever

A Seasonal Children's Favorite by Barbara Robinson

In Barbara Robinson's hilarious children's favorite, the traditional Christmas story takes a lively turn when the Herdman kids take the leading roles in the church pageant. It is, without a doubt, a Christmas pageant to remember! Share this outrageous, touching story with your students during the holiday season; then complement its reading with the following creative activities and reproducibles.

by Beth Gress

Ornamental Summaries

Highlight summarizing skills with a colorful, ongoing display. Reproduce page 99 on various colors of paper and provide each pair of students with two copies. After reading or listening to a chapter, have each pair write the chapter number in an ornament cap. Then instruct each pair of students to work together to write a brief summary of the chapter on the ornament. Use the ornaments as the border around a bulletin board, arrange them in a Christmas tree shape on a wall, or attach them to a class Christmas tree. After completing the book, have small groups brainstorm themes that represent the author's message. After sharing the themes, have the entire class select its top four. Write these themes on star patterns to place near the top of the tree or in the bulletin-board corners.

Name That Narrator

The Best Christmas Pageant Ever is told in first-person narration, yet readers must infer to learn the narrator's identity. As they listen to or read the book, challenge students to find out as much as they can about the story's narrator. Duplicate page 101 for students to use to record clues that lead them to their conclusions. For example, is the narrator a girl or a boy? How old is the narrator? What evidence in the story backs up these opinions? Have students follow the directions for completing the page.

The Gazette Tells All!

The Herdman kids get into big trouble, big enough to make front-page news in any small town! Using the reproducible on page 100, have students write front-page stories about the fire that burned down Fred Shoemaker's toolhouse. Remind students to use the journalistic style—answering the questions *who? what? when? where?* and *how?*—and to fill in logical information not mentioned in the story, such as Shoemaker's address. Have students illustrate their stories in the boxes and write eye-catching headlines on the bold lines. To complete the activity, have students add other events from the book or create additional news stories that might make headlines in this fictional town.

Behind The Scenes

The humorous antics of the Herdmans provide excellent opportunities for creative dramatics. Have students select and perform scenes, such as the "choosing roles" episode in chapter 3. Allow student groups time to write and practice their scenes, and then perform them for the rest of the class. Encourage each group to read dramatically and include appropriate gestures or improvisation.

For a role-playing twist, have students take on roles and improvise dialogue for events that are "behind the scenes" in the story. For example, have students role-play:

- the Herdman kids in the toolhouse playing with the chemistry set that they stole
- Imogene blackmailing kids at recess about knowing their weights
- Alice Wendleken reporting to her mother all of the terrible things that are going on at the rehearsals
- the ladies in the church kitchen preparing food and discussing the pageant
- the Herdmans and the librarian looking up information about King Herod and the Christmas story

Jackdaws

A *jackdaw* is a collection of items that represents a book. The term comes from the name of a common crow found in Europe and North Africa. Jackdaws like to collect and hide small, brightly colored objects. As a literature extension, the items in a jackdaw provide background about a book and stimulate student interest. Its contents, limited only by one's imagination and creativity, can include clothing, songs, news articles, maps, recipes, and trinkets—which may be real, replicated, or invented. Items in a jackdaw must be related to the book in a definite way.

As they read *The Best Christmas Pageant Ever*, have students choose items for their jackdaws at the end of each chapter. To help them get started, suggest an item from a chemistry set, a doughnut box, a cigar, a Bible, some angel wings, a tinsel halo, or a charm bracelet. (Allow students to include drawings if the actual items can't be found or are impractical to display.) Provide space in the classroom for students to arrange their jackdaw displays.

Map The Middle Eastern Trek

What was it like traveling to Bethlehem on a donkey? Why were Mary and Joseph traveling anyway, if Mary was "with child"? Where did their trip begin? Form small groups to research answers to these questions about the Christmas story. On a map of the Middle East, have students outline the route that Mary and Joseph may have followed, noting the distance that they traveled, how long the trip may have taken by donkey, and what the terrain and weather may have been like. Have students research the city of Bethlehem and find pictures of the city's many sacred, historical shrines.

Still-Life Illustrations

As a culminating activity after reading the book, have groups of students choose moments in the story to act out in frozen tableaux. At each group's turn, the members of the group go to the front of the classroom, introduce the characters they represent, and pose—in still-life fashion—in a moment from the story. The rest of the class tries to determine what moment in the story the group is portraying. As a comprehension check, ask each student/character a question about him- or herself. Or have other students question the role players. Use an instant camera to photograph these scenes; then arrange the photos on a bulletin board in the order in which they happened. Have each group write a caption to place under its photograph.

Journal Entries

Students always have a variety of reactions to the characters and events in *The Best Christmas Pageant Ever.* Have students write about any of the events listed in "Behind The Scenes" on page 97 as a script. Or suggest the following topics for journal entries:

- Create a letter that Mr. Herdman might write to his family years after he has left them.
- Create a letter that the Herdmans might write to their father if they learned of his whereabouts.
- Write a title for each chapter of the book.
- Write the list that Alice Wendleken might have written in her little notebook.
- Create a program that might have been distributed at the church pageant. Include a cast list, a song list, a note from the director, etc.
- Write excerpts from Imogene's diary—before, during, and after her participation in the Christmas pageant.
- Write an eighth chapter to the book, showing how the Herdmans' lives (or the narrator's life) might have changed as a result of the pageant.

TRDavidson

Note To The Teacher: Use this reproducible with other holiday writing projects and activities.

The Gazette

Vol.   No.   Date: Price:

Note To The Teacher: Use this reproducible with *"The Gazette* Tells All!" on page 97, or with other novels and literature selections. Or use it to make a student-written class newsletter.

As Told By...

Just who *is* the narrator? Sometimes it's hard to determine who's telling the story in a book. The narrator may be an observer of what's going on in the book, or he or she may be directly involved in the action. The narrator can even be an animal!

Use the following outline to help you describe the narrator in the book you are reading:

I. Is the narrator a male or a female? _____ Write clues
   that helped you to decide. _____
   _____

II. Is the narrator a child or an adult? _____ Write clues
   that helped you to decide. _____
   _____

III. What are some of the narrator's **actions** that give clues about his or her
   identity? _____
   _____

IV. What are some things that the narrator **says** that give clues about his or
   her identity? _____
   _____

V. Write a description of the narrator based on all of the clues you listed.
   _____
   _____

VI. Draw a picture of the narrator in the box.

Bonus Box: Choose another character from the book and write a description of him or her. Don't give the name of the character in the description. Give your description to a friend. Can your friend identify the character from reading your description?

©1998 The Education Center, Inc. • *The Best Of The Mailbox® Literature • Intermediate • TEC1464*

Note To The Teacher: Use this activity with "Name That Narrator" on page 97. It can also be used with any literature selection in which the first-person narrator is not named.

Hatchet

A Newbery Honor Book by Gary Paulsen

Lost in the Canadian wilderness with only his hatchet and a hunger for survival, Brian faces the biggest challenge of his young life—bigger even than the pain of his parents' divorce. Share the suspense of this heart-stopping adventure with your students; then use the following creative activities and reproducibles to extend this story of a boy's struggle for survival.

by Joy Ann Tweedt

An A+ Survival Attitude

Experts say that a survival attitude is the key element in most survival success stories. Before reading *Hatchet*, have students share survival stories they have heard. Provide old copies of *Reader's Digest* magazine, which regularly publishes survival stories. Have students read several stories and determine the attitudes or personality qualities that seem to make the characters in the story survivors (a will to live, determination, love of family, anger, stubbornness, etc.). List these characteristics on a large piece of chart paper to display in the classroom. Have students look for these attitudes in Brian as they read *Hatchet*.

Move Over, Oprah!

If anyone knows how much the public loves survival stories, it's talk show hosts! Let your students trade places with Phil, Oprah, Maury, and Geraldo with the following activity. Discuss how to develop good interview questions; then divide the class into two groups. On index cards, have one group write questions to ask Brian after he is rescued from the wilderness (one question per card). Have the other group write responses to the questions on a sheet of paper. Choose one student to be Brian; then give him a copy of the written responses to review. Choose another student to be the talk show host. Arrange your classroom to resemble a talk show set; then place Brian and the host in front of the rest of the students, or the "studio audience." Distribute the question cards to members of the audience. Videotape the talk show host introducing Brian and opening up the show to questions from the audience. For a really realistic show, have small groups of students plan commercials to perform during breaks.

Personal Response Writing

With its piercing look inside the heart and mind of a lone survivor, *Hatchet* is a perfect book for journal-writing activities. As students read, have them record their thoughts and feelings as if they were Brian. Encourage them to cite examples from the book to support their writings, and to reflect on their own personal experiences as well. Use the following journal starters to stimulate critical thinking:

- What would you have done differently if you had been Brian?
- A teacher once told Brian that *he* was his only asset and that he needed to be positive, get motivated, and stay on top of things. How does this advice affect Brian? What do you think of this advice?
- Suppose the pilot had lived. How might this have changed the story? How would this have changed Brian?
- Which event in the story would have been the most difficult for you to handle if you had been Brian?
- How did this survival experience change Brian physically and psychologically?
- Explain how a survival experience might be beneficial to a person.

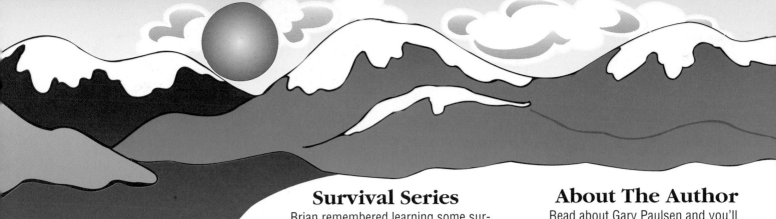

Tell Me There's A Sequel!

After experiencing the nonstop adventure of *Hatchet*, your students will be eager to follow up with another great survival tale. Ask students if they think Brian will ever return to his shelter on the L-shaped lake in Canada. For what purpose would he return? What ordeals might he face this time? Encourage interested students to read *The River* by Gary Paulsen to find out what happens when Brian returns to the Canadian wilderness. If students are still hungry for more survival stories, point them in the direction of these survival novels for young readers:

The Cay by Theodore Taylor
Island Of The Blue Dolphins
   by Scott O'Dell
The Sign Of The Beaver by Elizabeth
   G. Speare
Iceberg Hermit by Arthur Roth
Lost In The Devil's Desert
   by Gloria Skurzynski
Frozen Fire by James Houston
The Talking Earth by Jean C. George
Slake's Limbo by Felice Holman

Illustrated Timeline

First Meat Day, First Rabbit Day, First Arrow Day—Brian measured time by his survival successes. As a class, decide on 10 to 12 important events from the story. Have students work with partners to illustrate each of the events on a large piece of art paper. Instruct students to summarize the event in a caption written at the top or bottom of the illustration. Display the illustrations in order in a hallway for other classes to enjoy. Duplicate the hatchet pattern on page 104 on gray construction paper for each student. After cutting out his hatchet, have the student label it with his opinion about *Hatchet*. Mount the hatchet cutouts along the borders of the timeline.

Survival Series

Brian remembered learning some survival techniques from watching a television show. Have your class produce its own educational television series on survival. Divide students into several cooperative research teams. Explain that each group will be responsible for writing a script and videotaping a production on one of the following topics: Constructing A Shelter, Finding Water, Building A Fire, Trapping Animals, Identifying Edible Plants. To help students with their research, provide a Boy Scout field book and other titles on survival skills, such as the following:

Tom Brown's Field Guide To Nature
   And Survival For Children by Tom
   Brown, Jr., with Judy Brown
Survival Basics For Kids by Cindy
   Coble
Coping With Natural Disasters by
   Caroline Arnold

About The Author

Read about Gary Paulsen and you'll learn why his books have such a realistic, "almost-like-you're-there" quality to them. Paulsen has participated three times in the 1,049-mile Iditarod race from Anchorage to Nome, Alaska. He's been attacked by a moose, dragged by sled dogs, and has fallen through ice to what seemed certain death. His other Newbery Honor book, *Dogsong*, details some of these experiences. Many of Paulsen's books are built around a self-centered character who, suddenly thrust into a survival situation, must develop new attitudes and skills to survive. Paulsen has stated that his characters "aren't faced with easy, answerable questions, but some find inner peace." Other Paulsen books to sample include *Popcorn Days And Buttermilk Nights*, *The Crossing*, *The Island*, and *The Winter Room*.

Pattern

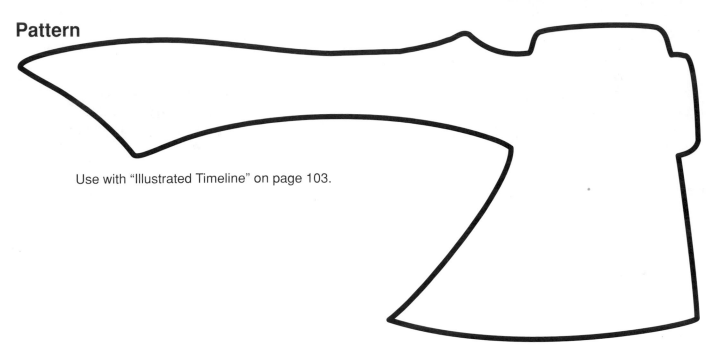

Use with "Illustrated Timeline" on page 103.

Note To The Teacher: Duplicate the cards below on construction paper; then cut them apart. Give one card to each of six student groups. Have each group discuss the passage from *Hatchet* on its card (see Student Instructions below). After 10 or 15 minutes, rotate the cards or have groups share what they have discussed.

Student Instructions: Locate the passage in your book and reread it carefully. Discuss the passage in your group. How does it relate to Brian and his experience in the wilderness? Why is it a significant passage? How can you apply this passage to your own life? What event or time in your life does this passage remind you of?

CHAPTER 2 "For a time that he could not understand Brian could do nothing. Even after his mind began working and he could see what had happened he could do nothing. It was as if his hands and arms were lead."	**CHAPTER 5** "...stay positive and stay on top of things. Brian thought of him now—wondered how to stay positive and stay on top of all this...'You are your most valuable asset. Don't forget that. *You* are the best thing you have.'"
CHAPTER 8 "...feeling sorry for yourself didn't work. It wasn't just that it was wrong to do, or that it was considered incorrect. It was more than that—it didn't work."	**CHAPTER 13** "...the Brian that stood and watched the wolves move away and nodded to them was completely changed. Time had come, time that he measured but didn't care about; time had come into his life and moved out and left him different.... Forty-two days, he thought, since he had died and been born as the new Brian."
CHAPTER 14 "Small mistakes could turn into disasters, funny little mistakes could snowball so that while you were still smiling at the humor you could find yourself looking at death."	**CHAPTER 15** "Patience, he thought. So much of this was patience— waiting and thinking and doing things right. So much of all this, so much of all living was patience and thinking."

Name_____

Old Brian, New Brian

After his incredible struggle for survival, Brian was definitely *not* the same person he was before the crash. Think about what you picture or what the author told you about the "old" Brian. Then think about how Brian's experiences in the wilderness changed him. Write your thoughts in the boxes below.

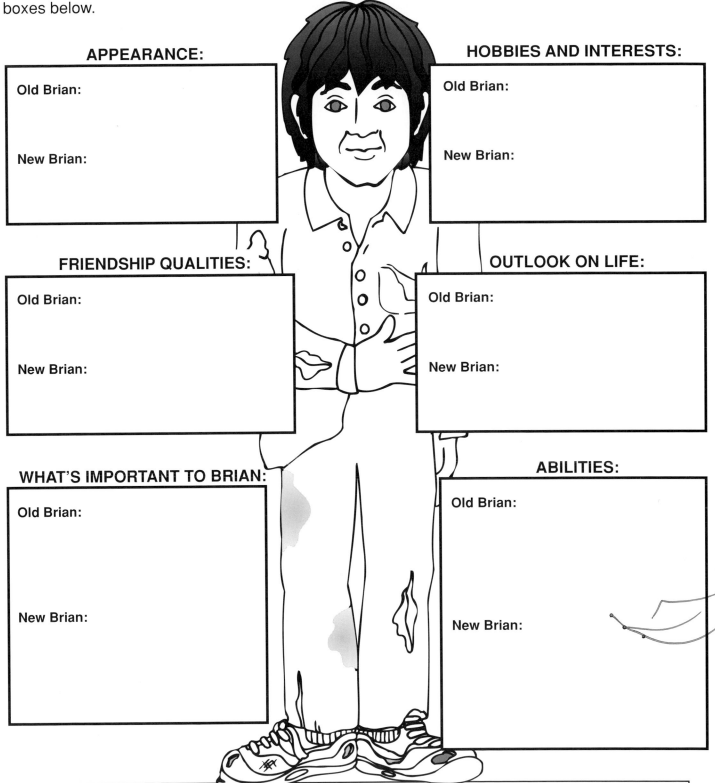

APPEARANCE:

Old Brian:

New Brian:

HOBBIES AND INTERESTS:

Old Brian:

New Brian:

FRIENDSHIP QUALITIES:

Old Brian:

New Brian:

OUTLOOK ON LIFE:

Old Brian:

New Brian:

WHAT'S IMPORTANT TO BRIAN:

Old Brian:

New Brian:

ABILITIES:

Old Brian:

New Brian:

Bonus Box: If you could award a medal to Brian for any one thing he did or accomplished while in the wilderness, what would you honor him for? On another piece of paper, design a certificate that honors Brian for that accomplishment.

A Walk In Brian's Shoes

Decisions in survival situations can be a matter of life or death. Brian Robeson knew how small mistakes could turn into disasters, so he tried to learn from his mistakes.

On the left of the chart are some of Brian's actions. Beside each action, write what you would do in the same situation now that you've learned from Brian's experience.

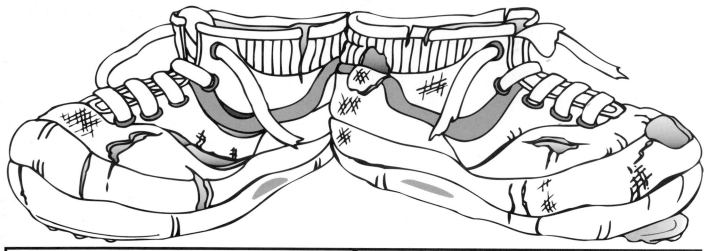

WHAT BRIAN DID	WHAT I MIGHT DO
• decided to fly the plane until it ran out of gas	
• buried the turtle eggs in his shelter	
• went back to the raspberry bushes even after seeing the bear	
• kicked and threw his hatchet at the sound in his shelter (a porcupine)	
• threw a handful of sand at a skunk	
• tried to get out of the water quickly after the moose attacked him	
• never discussed "The Secret" with his mother or father	

Bonus Box: On the back of this page, make a list entitled "Ten Things To Remember About Survival." Compare your list with the list of a partner in your class.

THE WESTING GAME
An Intriguing Whodunit

Who killed Sam Westing? Is he really dead? Tantalize your students with this clever Newbery Medal–winning mystery by Ellen Raskin.

by Beth Gress

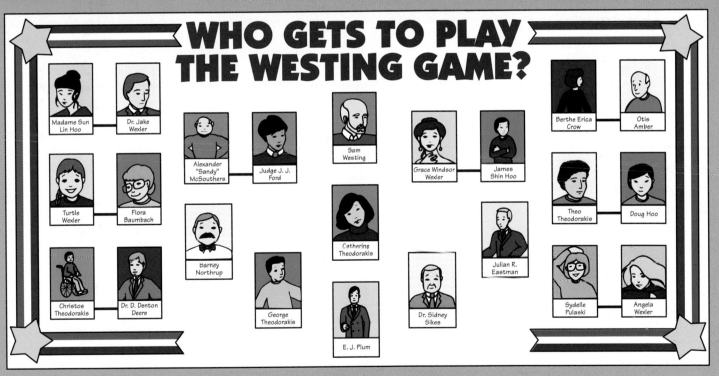

WHO GETS TO PLAY THE WESTING GAME?

Madame Sun Lin Hoo — Dr. Jake Wexler

Alexander "Sandy" McSouthers — Judge J. J. Ford

Sam Westing

Grace Windsor Wexler — James Shin Hoo

Berthe Erica Crow — Otis Amber

Turtle Wexler — Flora Baumbach

Barney Northrup

Catherine Theodorakis

Theo Theodorakis — Doug Hoo

Christos Theodorakis — Dr. D. Denton Deere

George Theodorakis

Dr. Sidney Sikes

Julian R. Eastman

Sydelle Pulaski — Angela Wexler

E. J. Plum

Who Gets To Play The Westing Game?

Keeping up with all the different characters in *The Westing Game* is loads of fun, but can be a bit confusing. Have your students make a display that keeps readers straight on who's who. Collect magazines that contain photos of people. After your class has read the first seven chapters, pass out piles of magazines to small groups of students. Instruct groups to use the story clues to select photos that could represent the story characters. Once every group has selected a photo for each character, have the class vote on the picture they think best represents each character. Arrange the pictures on a bulletin board with the portraits grouped according to their Westing Game partnerships (see the illustration).

Keeping Case Notes

Tracking clues in *The Westing Game* will be easier—and even more fun—if students work together in groups. Supply each group with one copy of the book and two copies of the "Case Notes" reproducible on page 110. As you or the students read the book, instruct groups to record each character's name and information about him/her on the reproducible. (Refer students to the bulletin board described on page 107 to help them list the characters.) Give each group a folder in which to store its case notes.

How will you keep curious students from reading ahead and spoiling the fun for more patient readers? Each day—before handing out the books to each group—secure the pages you don't want students to read by putting a rubber band around them from top to bottom. Discourage students from peeking ahead by telling them that they may not remove the rubber bands from their books.

SKIES AM SHINING BROTHER

HIS N ON TO THEE FOR

Who's The Quicker Picker-Upper?

Which of your students will figure out the clues first? Help your student groups search for the solution to the mystery in the same way that the characters do. In the story, the Westing Game clues are written on squares cut from paper towels. Cut several paper towels into two-inch squares. Give each group six to eight of the squares and one whole paper-towel sheet. As they read, have students use felt-tipped markers to write the clue words given in the story onto the squares. Post the clue word squares on the bulletin board (page 107) next to the game partners. As clue words are added to the display, have groups try to figure out the meaning of the clues. Prior to reading chapter 17, have each group submit the solution (written on the whole paper towel) it thinks is most likely. After completing the book, compare the actual solution to the students' predictions.

Journal Topics And More!

Chapter titles often give clues to upcoming events, and those in *The Westing Game* are no exception. At the beginning of each chapter, have students predict what will occur according to the chapter title. After reading the chapter, discuss how the title related to the events in the chapter.

In addition to looking at the titles, encourage students to reflect on and react to each section of the story by responding to the following thought-provoking journal questions:

Ch. 2: What would it take for you to volunteer to do what Turtle did?

Ch. 4: What would you do if you had found the body like Turtle did?

Ch. 7: Who is your favorite character so far? Why?

Ch. 8: What would you do with the $10,000?

Ch. 9: What notice might you put up in the elevator?

Ch. 11: Choose one pair of game partners and explain why they make perfect partners.

Ch. 13: Choose three characters and give reasons why each might have set off the bomb.

Ch. 22: Write the words to "America, The Beautiful" or some other patriotic song. Explain what the words mean to you.

Ch. 25: Do you think Berthe Erica Crow is guilty or innocent? What evidence can you give to support your view?

End: Who would you say is the hero of *The Westing Game?* Why? Is there a villain in the story? If so, who is it?

Who Am I?

I don't go by my real name most of the story.

I have a small room.

I play the stock market.

I kick shins.

I have a long braid.

Answer: Turtle Wexler

Who Am I?

Use the many characters of *The Westing Game* to make up a Who Am I? game. Write each character's name on a slip of paper. (See the bulletin board on page 107 for a complete listing of characters.) Then have each student draw one name. Instruct the student to write five clues about the identity of his character on an index card, listing them from the hardest clue to the easiest clue. Collect and shuffle the clue cards; then divide the class into four teams. Read the top clue from a card to the first team. After the team has collaborated, instruct a spokesman to tell you the team's guess. Award points based on the number of clues needed to guess the solution. For example, if the team guesses correctly after only one clue, it wins five points. If only two clues are read, the team wins four points, and so on. After one team has guessed from a card, move to the next team, using a new card. After all the cards have been read, tally the points to determine the winning team.

Follow The Stocks

Turtle Wexler convinced Flora Baumbach that the best way to invest their $10,000 was to play the stock market. Explore the stock market with your class by having cooperative groups select three well-known stocks to follow for the duration of the unit. Divide the class into five groups. Give each group a copy of stock quotes from the business section of the daily newspaper and a copy of "Staking Out The Stocks" on page 112. (Two well-known places that register and list stocks are the New York Stock Exchange [NYSE] and the American Stock Exchange [AMEX].) Help students locate some of the better-known stocks. Then have them use the information in "Staking Out The Stocks" to help them determine the price of their chosen stocks and how to keep track of daily changes in price.

If desired, make a class poster tracking each of the groups' stocks. Then have each group create a line graph plotting the rise or fall of its stocks during the unit. Post these line graphs with the stock report poster.

Have A Clue?

Teach your students the board game Clue®, and you'll teach them note-taking, organization, and logical-thinking skills. Have students compare Clue® to *The Westing Game* story. Which characters from Clue® do *The Westing Game* characters resemble? Discuss the similarities between the clue cards in the game and the paper-towel squares in the story. Expand this connection by having student groups create their own mystery board games using Clue® and *The Westing Game* as models. Provide pizza boxes for gameboards. Instruct students to include a background story, a cast of characters, game cards, playing pieces, and directions. Trade the completed games among the groups for playing.

Name(s) _____

110

Case Notes

Can you figure out who killed Sam Westing? Record what you discover about each character on two copies of this sheet. Then put together the clues to solve the mystery. Perhaps *you'll* be the winner of The Westing Game!

Character	Family	Occupation	Westing Game Partner	Other Information	Paper-Towel Clues

©1998 The Education Center, Inc. • *The Best Of The Mailbox® Literature • Intermediate •* TEC1464

Note To The Teacher: Duplicate two copies for each group or individual student. Use with "Keeping Case Notes" on page 108.

Money-Making Quotes

As you read *The Westing Game,* look for the following quotations. You'll find the speakers' names written on the stock market ticker tape around the page. As you figure out a quotation, cross off the portions of the name that are on the tape. Then rearrange the remaining letters to uncover a revealing message. Write the message in the box.

Gra   outhers   ber   ge   row   He   Wex   Jud   gela   ler   ca

1. _____ "Hi, Sandy, I won!"

2. _____ "I am the answer and I am the winner. I give half of my
inheritance to Otis Amber, to be used for the Good Salvation Soup Kitchen. I give
the rest of the money to Angela."

3. _____ "My mother was a servant in the Westing household,
my father worked for the railroad and was the gardener on his days off."

4. _____ "I'm no fool, you know. I knew I couldn't trust any one
of you. You can't read my shorthand because I wrote in Polish."

5. _____ "But Crow still needs me, and I'll stick by her no matter
what. I've grown fond of the woman; we've been together such a long time."

6. _____ "I'll hem your witch's costume, Turtle."

7. _____ "What a lovely living room, so practically furnished.
Our apartments are identical in layout, but mine looks so different. You must
come see what I've done with it. I'm a decorator, you know."

8. _____ "I can take some credit for those paper innersoles.
My feet were killing me, standing at the door all day, so I said to Jimmy: 'Jimmy,
if only somebody would invent a good innersole that didn't take up so much room
like those foam-rubber things.' And sure enough, he did it. They're great, I got a
pair in my shoes now, wanna see?"

Bonus Box: Find three
other important quotes in
the book. Write each quote
on a separate piece of paper (without identifying the
speaker). Write your name
on the back of each slip;
then give the slips to your
teacher to read aloud to the
class. How many of your
classmates can identify the
speakers of your quotes?

C laski is An J. J. no Ber delle dy Ford We Otis Eri

Sy t xler Am de the McS Wex ad tle San Pu

The hidden message:
_____

ce   Tur   ler

Note To The Teacher: Use this reproducible after students have read the book.   111

The Last Word

Now that you've finished reading *The Westing Game,* choose one list of words below. On your own paper, define each word. Then use the words to write a paragraph about the topic described below that list.

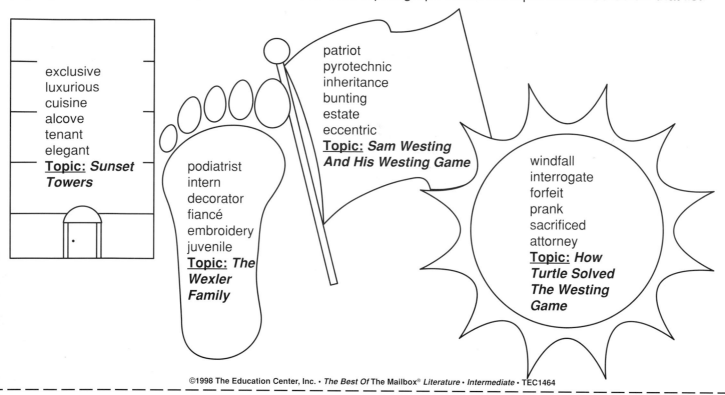

exclusive
luxurious
cuisine
alcove
tenant
elegant
Topic: *Sunset Towers*

patriot
pyrotechnic
inheritance
bunting
estate
eccentric
Topic: *Sam Westing And His Westing Game*

podiatrist
intern
decorator
fiancé
embroidery
juvenile
Topic: *The Wexler Family*

windfall
interrogate
forfeit
prank
sacrificed
attorney
Topic: *How Turtle Solved The Westing Game*

©1998 The Education Center, Inc. • *The Best Of* The Mailbox® *Literature* • *Intermediate* • TEC1464

Staking Out The Stocks

Turtle and Baba successfully invested their $10,000 in the stock market. How well do you think you can do? Use the chart below to help you read the stock listings. Then keep a ten-day account of three of your favorite stocks to see how well you might have done if you had played The Westing Game.

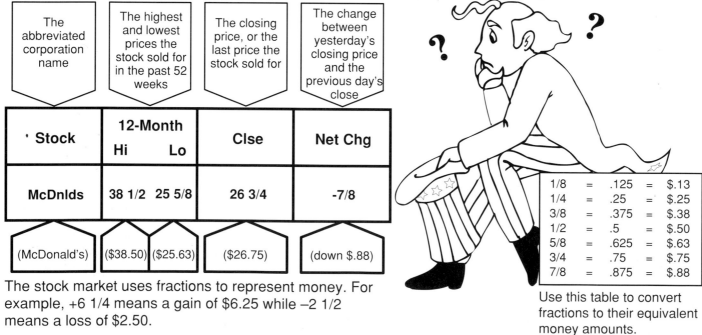

Stock	12-Month Hi Lo	Clse	Net Chg
The abbreviated corporation name	The highest and lowest prices the stock sold for in the past 52 weeks	The closing price, or the last price the stock sold for	The change between yesterday's closing price and the previous day's close
McDnlds	38 1/2 25 5/8	26 3/4	-7/8
(McDonald's)	($38.50) ($25.63)	($26.75)	(down $.88)

1/8	=	.125	=	$.13
1/4	=	.25	=	$.25
3/8	=	.375	=	$.38
1/2	=	.5	=	$.50
5/8	=	.625	=	$.63
3/4	=	.75	=	$.75
7/8	=	.875	=	$.88

The stock market uses fractions to represent money. For example, +6 1/4 means a gain of $6.25 while −2 1/2 means a loss of $2.50.

Use this table to convert fractions to their equivalent money amounts.

©1998 The Education Center, Inc. • *The Best Of* The Mailbox® *Literature* • *Intermediate* • TEC1464

Walk Two Moons
A Bittersweet Tale Of Love, Loss, Humor, And Suspense

In this 1995 Newbery Medal winner by Sharon Creech, 13-year-old Salamanca Tree Hiddle desperately wants to complete her cross-country journey to Idaho with her grandparents. Sal keeps the journey lively with tales of her friend Phoebe, the eccentric Mrs. Cadaver, and mysterious notes left by a "potential lunatic." Through her tales, Sal reveals pieces of her own life and hopes of finding her own mother, who left for Idaho promising to return. Upon reaching her final destination, Sal realizes she must accept the past, deal with the present, and look forward to the future. Extend this wonderful tale of self-discovery with the following creative activities.

by Lori Sammartino

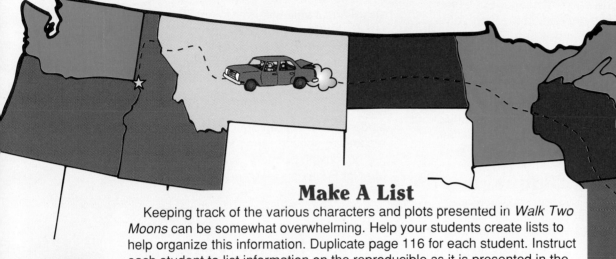

Make A List

Keeping track of the various characters and plots presented in *Walk Two Moons* can be somewhat overwhelming. Help your students create lists to help organize this information. Duplicate page 116 for each student. Instruct each student to list information on the reproducible as it is presented in the story. Periodically divide the students into small groups and have them compare their lists. Encourage each group member to add any information that he didn't previously have listed on his reproducible.

Call It Courage

After reading chapter 3, introduce *courage* as a recurrent theme in the story line. Construct a class chart to keep track of characters, their courageous acts, and the chapters in which the courageous acts can be found in the novel. Have students fill in the chart with information from the first three chapters; then continue to add to the chart for the remainder of the book. This chart will be a great reference to use with "Badge Of Courage" on page 115.

Courage Chart		
Character's Name	Courageous Act	Chapter
Sal	Picks up a spider	3
Gramps and the boy	Tend to Gram after she is bitten by a water moccasin	15
Phoebe	Shows the notes to the police	29

On The Road Again

Sharpen your students' geography skills by having them track Sal's journey from Ohio to Idaho. Post a large map of the United States on a bulletin board. Have students create and post a different symbol for each city and landmark Sal visits on the map. Connect the symbols with yarn to symbolize the route Sal takes to Idaho. Also have students research each famous landmark Sal visits such as the Black Hills, Mount Rushmore, and Old Faithful. After Sal reaches Idaho, have the students estimate how many miles she traveled since leaving Ohio. Then have them use the map's mileage scale to figure out how close their estimates are to the actual mileage.

"Don't judge a man until you've walked two moons in his moccasins."

Mystery Messages

Who's leaving the mysterious messages at Phoebe's front door? Have your junior sleuths construct Mystery Message Albums in which to collect and decode each message. Each time a mystery message appears in the story, give each student a 3" x 5" index card. Instruct the student to write the message on the front of the card, then write her interpretation of it on the back. Punch a hole in the upper left-hand corner of each card and give the student a twist-tie to bind the cards together. Have students read aloud and discuss their interpretations of each message.

Character Cinquains

Sal's teacher, Mr. Birkway, uses poetry to show his students how people can interpret things differently. Have each student write a *cinquain,* a five-line poem, that describes a favorite main character. Explain that the first line should contain the character's name; the second line, two adjectives; the third line, three verbs ending in *-ing;* the fourth line, the student's opinion of the character; and the fifth line, the character's title or position. Give each student a piece of white paper and markers. Instruct him to illustrate a character at the top of his sheet and write a cinquain about him or her at the bottom. Have each student read his cinquain to the class. Then discuss the students' interpretations of the characters.

Forget-Me-Not Box

In chapter 30, Sal reveals special items she has kept as reminders of her mom, such as a red shawl and a yellow-flowered cotton dress. Have your students create their own special forget-me-not boxes of special items that remind them of parents, grandparents, siblings, or friends. Duplicate page 117 for each student. Have students use this reproducible as a planning sheet for their forget-me-not boxes. Schedule a Forget-Me-Not Friday on which each student can share her forget-me-not box with her classmates.

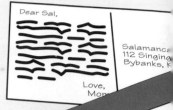

Dear Sal,

Salamanca
112 Singing
Bybanks, K

Love,
Mom

My Journa
Phoebe
Winterbotto

Double Take

Have you ever taken a second look at something and realized you missed seeing it? Mr. Birkway teaches his class about *perception* by showing his students a special picture. Some students immediately see a vase, while others see two heads or both. To further investigate this idea, read aloud *Round Trip* by Ann Jonas (Greenwillow Books, 1983). Read the book once; then flip it over and read it again. Students will experience a different perspective of the same book. Conclude this activity by having each child create an original picture that can be viewed in more than one way. Display the pictures on a bulletin board so students can view one another's work and try to identify the different perceptions.

Mr. Birkway
Dramatic, energetic
Bouncing, leaping, inspiring
A strange man who loves his job
Teacher

by Brianna

What If?

In chapter 41, Sal begins to wonder how her life would have been different if certain things had never happened. Have your students ponder similar thought-provoking questions as they play the What If game. Give each student a small index card on which to write a question that begins with "What if…." Provide students with examples such as "What if kids under 16 were allowed to drive?" or "What if a fifth grader became president?" Put all the cards in a bag; then have each student pull out one card, read the question aloud, and respond to it in front of the class. What a great way to get kids thinking fast on their feet!

Badge Of Courage
Presented
to
Sal
for the courage it took to drive herself to Lewiston.

Badge Of Courage

Honor the courageous characters of *Walk Two Moons* by having each student create a badge of courage. Tell the student to think of one character he feels is the most courageous. Remind students to use their courage chart from "Call It Courage" (page 113) as a guide in selecting a character. Provide each student with colored paper, markers, glitter, sequins, glue, and scissors for creating a badge. Instruct each student to include the character's name and a few sentences explaining why this character deserves the badge. Have each student present his badge of courage to the class; then post the badges around the room for all to enjoy.

Mrs. Cadaver's Confession

Mrs. Cadaver reveals her connection to Sal's parents in chapter 43. Have students reflect back to when Sal knew very little about Mrs. Cadaver. Discuss why Sal refused to talk about the woman with her father. Then have each student write a letter to Sal from Mrs. Cadaver explaining how she came to know Sal's parents. After each student has completed a rough draft, reread the descriptions of Mrs. Cadaver found in chapters 14 and 30 to help students gain more insight into her hobbies and interests. Then have each student create stationery that reflects Mrs. Cadaver's personality. Instruct each student to write the final copy of his letter on the stationery he created. Conclude by having each student read his letter to the rest of the class and explain the stationery's design.

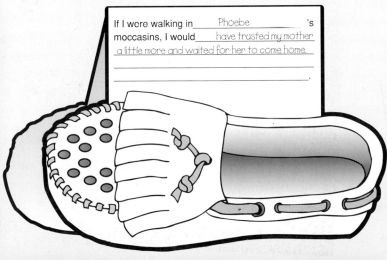

If I were walking in _____Phoebe_____'s moccasins, I would ___have trusted my mother a little more and waited for her to come home.___

Moccasin Walkers

At the end of the story, Sal and her grandfather pretend to walk in other people's moccasins. Have your students do the same by thinking about what it would be like to walk in the moccasins of two characters from the story. Duplicate the moccasin pattern on page 118 for each student. Instruct each student to cut out the pattern. For added strength, have each student glue his pattern onto a piece of tagboard, let it dry, and cut out the pattern again. Tell the student to fill out each side of the pattern for a different character. Encourage the student to decorate each moccasin based on the personality of its character, then fold the pattern along the dotted line. Display the moccasins around the room.

Listen And List

As you listen to and/or read *Walk Two Moons,* list information, words, and clues under each of the five categories below. Keep this page in a safe place so that you can add and refer to it often.

Ways Sal And Phoebe Are Alike:

Things Sal Remembers About Her Mom:

Interesting Words:

Main Characters:

Places Sal And Her Grandparents Visit:

Bonus Box: On the back of this page, create a wish list that Sal might have written at the end of the novel.

Forget-Me-Not Box

In *Walk Two Moons*, Salamanca mentions special items she keeps beneath the floorboards in her room to remind her of her mother. Now it's your turn to collect items you can use to make a forget-me-not box to honor someone special like your mom, dad, a brother or sister, another relative, or even a friend.

Directions: Answer the following questions to help you plan your forget-me-not box.

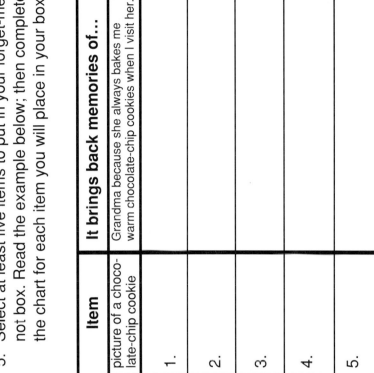

5. Select at least five items to put in your forget-me-not box. Read the example below; then complete the chart for each item you will place in your box.

Item	It brings back memories of...
picture of a choco-late-chip cookie	Grandma because she always bakes me warm chocolate-chip cookies when I visit her.
1.	
2.	
3.	
4.	
5.	

1. What is the name of the person I've chosen to honor with a forget-me-not box? _____

2. How am I related to this person? _____

3. Why is this person special to me? _____
_____

4. What type of box will I use for my forget-me-not box? _____

   How will I decorate it? _____
_____

Bonus Box: On the back of this page, list five items that your special person might pick if he or she created a forget-me-not box to remember you. Then briefly explain why these items might be in the box.

Note To The Teacher: Use with "Forget-Me-Not Box" on page 114.

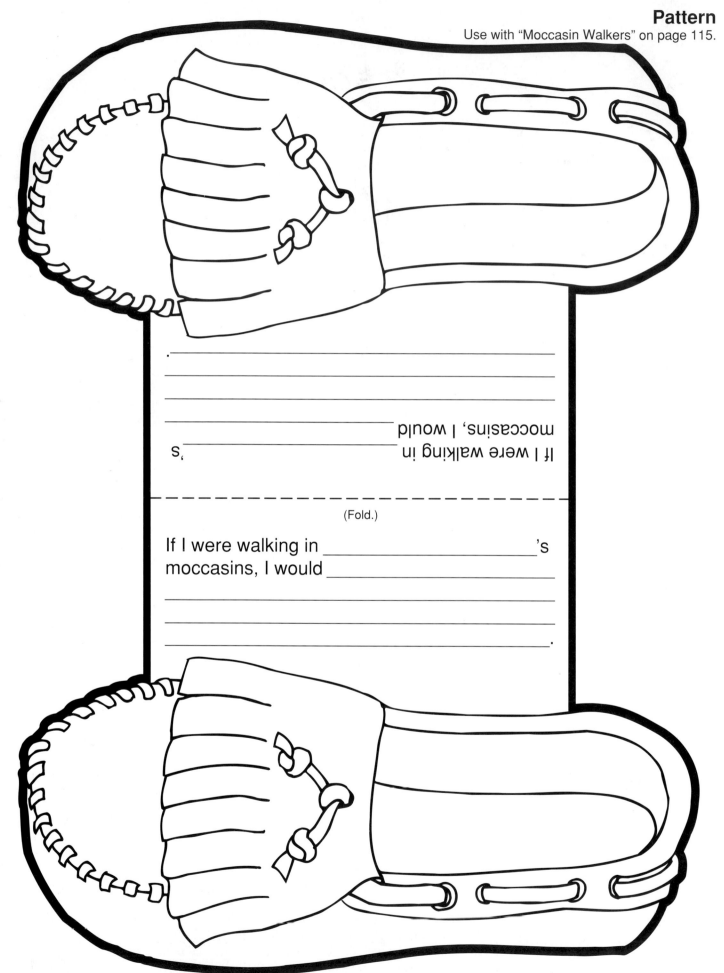

If I were walking in _____'s
moccasins, I would _____
_____
_____
_____ .

(Fold.)

The Trumpet Of The Swan
A Children's Classic By E. B. White

This classic tale of a mute trumpeter swan named Louis speaks directly and delightfully to every child who's realized with horror that he's somehow different. Cheer as Louis triumphs over his handicap to win fame, fortune, and the love of the beautiful Serena; then soar to new learning heights with these creative activities and reproducibles that extend E. B. White's masterpiece.

with contributions by Mary Anne Haffner

Setting The Stage

Louis starts his rather unusual life on a pond deep in the Canadian forest. Use this marvelous fantasy to introduce a lesson on pond/wetland habitats. Provide students with books and other resource information about forest wetlands. Cut through one corner of a large appliance box to make a large, folded mural panel. Have one group of students research, sketch, and paint a forest wetland scene on the panel. Next have each student or pair of students research a wetland animal (see the list below); then have the students draw and cut out pictures of their animals to mount on the mural. Provide time for students to share their research on the wetlands animals. Stand the completed mural in a corner of the room; then add a few soft pillows to make a cozy corner for silent or shared reading of *The Trumpet Of The Swan*.

muskrat	moose
beaver	otter
red-winged blackbird	woodpecker
mosquito	Canada goose
chipmunk	sparrow
bullfrog	mallard duck
chickadee	striped skunk
marsh wren	raccoon
red fox	snowshoe hare

Separating Fact From Fiction

In his fantasy about Louis, author E. B. White includes factual information about trumpeter swans. But how accurate is White's information? Ask your media specialist to provide information on swans duplicated from encyclopedias, bird field guides, and other resource books. After reading each of the first four chapters of *The Trumpet Of The Swan*, list as a class any facts about trumpeter swans on a large piece of chart paper; then ask students if they think White's information is accurate. How can they be sure? Divide students into groups; then give each group copies of the resource information about swans. Assign each group the task of using the information to verify the accuracy of several facts on the class list. Have groups share their findings with the rest of the class.

After this exercise, discuss how E. B. White's research on trumpeter swans added appeal to his book. How might the book have been different without the factual information on swans? To extend this activity, have each student choose a particular animal to research for several days. After each student keeps a log of facts about his animal, have him write a short fictional story about his animal, weaving some of his factual information into the tale just as E. B. White did.

Buddy Up!

Louis's human buddy, Sam Beaver, writes nightly in a journal, concluding each entry with a question so that he will have something to think about while falling asleep. Often he includes an illustration with his text. Stimulate student writing with this "buddy up" journal activity. Duplicate two copies of the swan booklet cover on page 121 on white construction paper for each student. After cutting out the covers, have each student trace one copy of the cover onto several sheets of lined notebook paper and cut out the tracings. Have students decorate their front and back covers, then staple these lined pages between them. Provide class time for students to write responses to each day's reading of *The Trumpet Of The Swan*. Challenge students to end each day's entry with a question, similar to Sam's. During the next day's writing period, have each student switch journals with a buddy. Have the buddy write a response to his partner's question; then have partners share their responses with each other.

Overcomers, Inc.

"Remember that the world is full of youngsters who have some sort of handicap that they must overcome. I am sure you will overcome it, in time." So speaks Louis's father as he confronts his young son with the disturbing news that he can't speak. It will be a rare student who doesn't identify in some way with Louis's uneasiness at discovering he's "different." Discuss with students how Louis must have felt at not being able to speak and the positive attitude he developed about his handicap. What are some obstacles that your students have overcome with hard work and a positive attitude? Challenge students to begin searching in newspapers and magazines for examples of inspiring overcomers. Set aside a small bulletin board entitled "Overcomers, Inc." on which students can post articles about people who have surmounted challenging handicaps. In addition, encourage students to add to the display brief notes of praise recognizing friends or relatives who they think should be honored as overcomers.

Let Me Toot My Horn About...

For an easy student-made display, draw a simple horn pattern (see the example on page 123); then duplicate copies of it on yellow construction paper. Have student volunteers cut out the horns and store them in a shoebox. On a bulletin board, mount the title "Toot Your Horn About…." Every few days post a large index card labeled with one of the sentence endings listed below. During free time, let each student label a horn with his opinion about the statement posted on the bulletin board. Set aside time to review and discuss the opinions expressed on the display. After the discussion, take down the horns and post a new ending.

Let me toot my horn about...
- what Sam might be when he grows up.
- Sam's practice of writing in a journal every night.
- the way that Louis's father told Louis about his "defect."
- whether Louis's father was right in saying that "the world is full of talkers, but it is rare to find anyone who listens."
- Mr. Brickle's statement that "everyone is entitled to his likes and dislikes and to his prejudices."
- the fact that Sam never told his father about Louis and the trumpeter swans.
- whether Louis's father did the right thing in stealing the trumpet.
- whether it is frightening to be different from everyone else.

National Geographic Presents...

If the adventures of Louis had actually happened, you can bet that *National Geographic* would have been right on top of the story! For a fun culminating activity, divide your class into several "investigative teams." Tell students to pretend that they work for the National Geographic Society. Each group has been asked to create a brief television program about Louis. Before setting groups free to begin planning their presentations, discuss features that might be included in a program about Louis. How about interviews with Sam Beaver, Mrs. Hammerbotham, Mr. Brickle of Camp Kookooskoos, and the manager of the Ritz Hotel? Or an "on-location" visit to the pond where Louis was born or the music store that Louis's father robbed? After groups have practiced their programs, videotape each team's presentation. Then pop some popcorn and invite a neighboring class to join yours for an afternoon of viewing enjoyment.

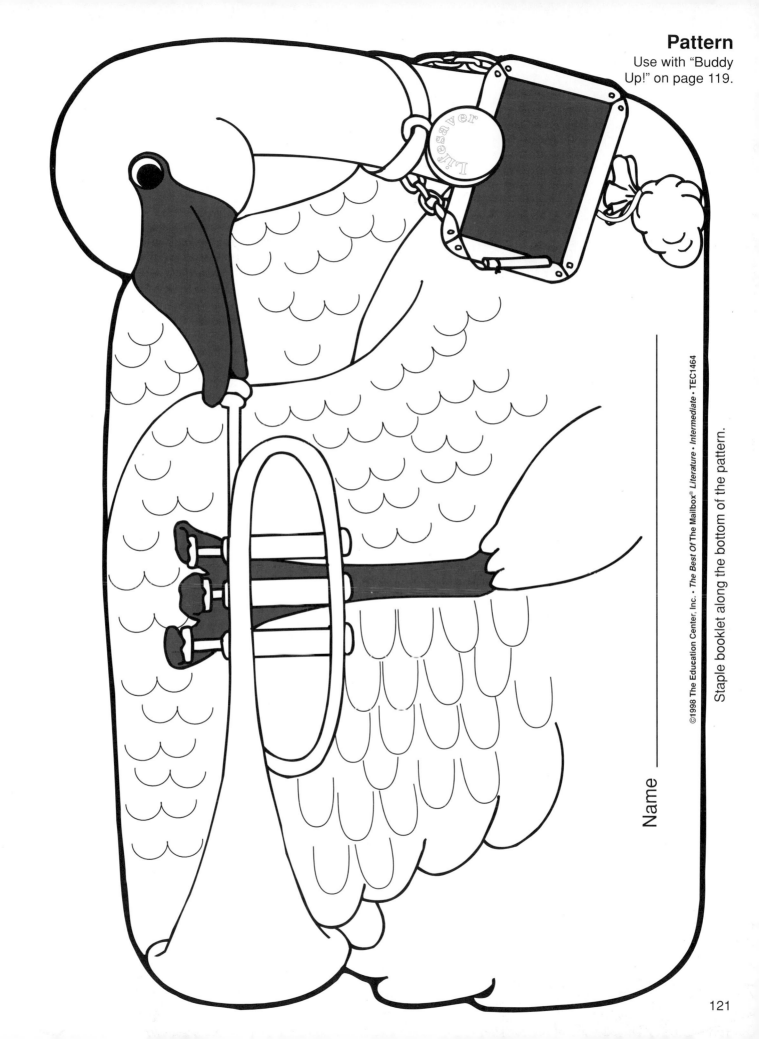

Name _____

Staple booklet along the bottom of the pattern.

Nothing Like A Twosome!

There's nothing like a twosome—just ask Louis and Serena! So join with a partner to complete this activity.

Directions:
1. Fill in the blanks to create a set of questions about *The Trumpet Of The Swan*.
2. When you are finished, switch papers with another twosome; then discuss the questions with your partner.
3. Choose three questions; then write the answers on the back of the paper.
4. Return the questions to the twosome who wrote them.

a. How are _____ and _____ alike?

b. How are _____ and _____ different?

c. Do you think it was right or wrong for _____
_____ ?

d. What caused Louis to _____ ?

e. What word best describes the way Louis _____
_____ ?

f. What are examples of _____ in the story?

g. Why do you think Louis _____
_____ ?

h. How did _____ affect _____
_____ ?

i. What was the most important _____
_____ ?

j. If you were the author, would you have _____
_____ ?

k. How did _____ change during the story?

l. What might have happened if _____
_____ ?

Note To The Teacher: If desired, use the questions written by students in this exercise in whole-class or small-group discussions.

Name_____

Take Note!

Directions:

1. Choose any four cards below.
2. Cut out the cards; then glue them to the front of a large string-tie envelope.
3. Complete each activity. Store your work inside the envelope.
4. Turn in your envelope on

_____.
due date

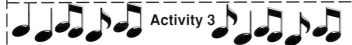 **Activity 1**

Cover a box with gift wrap. Choose a character from the book; then cut out pictures of gifts appropriate for that character from old magazines or catalogs. Glue the pictures onto the gift box. Include a greeting card that explains the selection of each gift.

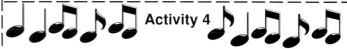 **Activity 2**

Draw a scene from the book. Glue the picture to tagboard; then cut the picture into puzzle pieces. Store the pieces in a Ziploc® bag. Give the puzzle to a classmate to reassemble.

Activity 3

Louis carried his possessions around his neck. Design a necklace or charm bracelet with symbols of the possessions you would carry if you were Louis. On a separate index card, include reasons for choosing each item.

Activity 4

Pretend to be a main character from the book. Write a letter to your readers thanking them for sharing your adventures. Include information about what happens to you after the novel ends.

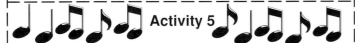 **Activity 5**

A male swan is a *cob*, while a baby is a *cygnet*. Make a chart listing different kinds of animals. List the names of the male, female, and baby of each species.

 **Activity 6**

Create a travel brochure that invites adventurers to camp in the Red Lakes National Wildlife Refuge in Montana and study the wildlife.

 **Activity 7**

Design a product that could be used by one of the characters in the novel.

Activity 8

Write a newspaper article about one of the following events in the story. Be sure to include the five *Ws*: *What? Where? When? Why? Who?*

- Louis's father crashing into the music store and stealing the trumpet
- Louis learning to read and write in Mrs. Hammerbotham's class
- Louis's rescue of Applegate Skinner
- Louis's job in Boston with the Swan Boat
- The return of Louis's father to the music store with money to reimburse the owner

---

Note To The Teacher: Fill in the due date above before duplication. Provide each student with a copy of this reproducible, a pair of scissors, glue, and a string-tie envelope.

My Side Of The Mountain
A Story Of Wilderness Survival And Adventure

Surviving in the wilderness with only $40, a penknife, twine, an ax, and some flint and steel seems an insurmountable task. But in her novel *My Side Of The Mountain*, Jean Craighead George reveals how young Sam Gribley does just that after running away from his crowded New York City home. Bring this wonderful story of courage and survival to life with the following creative activities.

with ideas by Lauren Medve and Patricia Altmann

Setting The Stage

Unless your students live near or have visited the Catskill Mountains, they may not be familiar with the setting of this novel. Gather atlases, almanacs, encyclopedias, and other references on the region; then divide your students into groups of four. Have each group research the following questions prior to reading the story:

1. In what state are the Catskill Mountains located?
2. What are the approximate degrees of longitude and latitude of the Catskills?
3. What is the climate of the Catskills like?
4. How do the people who live in the Catskills year-round prepare for the winter months?
5. Would you like to live in the Catskills? Why or why not? Support your answers with facts from your research.

Picture The Setting

As students read *My Side Of The Mountain,* have them pay close attention to the author's detailed description of Sam's new home. Encourage each student to record specific details in his reading journal. Next provide each child with a sheet of art paper and colored pencils. Direct each student to use details he recorded in his journal to draw Sam's tree house. Have small groups compare their drawings before posting the pictures on a bulletin board.

Flashback!

My Side Of The Mountain is a great resource for introducing the literary technique of flashback. A *flashback* is "a break in text that describes an event or a scene from the past." As you read chapter 1, instruct students to look for the change in time that occurs when the story switches from a flashback about Sam writing in his journal about Baron to the present time, which is a year later. Similarly, have students look for the time shift in chapter 2 that begins with the flashback of Sam leaving his New York City home heading for the Catskills. After students have seen how a flashback can be used to capture reader interest, have each child write a brief autobiography that begins with a flashback of an interesting event from her past.

Tom

Sam's Tree Home
- hollowed out
- fireplace made of clay and rocks
- bed made with an ash slat

Fishing For Meaning

Reading a story without understanding its vocabulary is like fishing without a pole—you just don't have what you need to get the job done! Make sure your students have the comprehension tools they need by creating a *My Side Of The Mountain* vocabulary bulletin board. Provide each student with a fish pattern cut from colorful construction paper; then assign her one word from the list below. Instruct the student to write the word and its definition on the fish pattern and add a colorful illustration. Attach each completed fish to a bulletin board titled "Fishing For Meaning." Add more fish to the display as your students encounter other unfamiliar words in the book.

Chapters 1–3: exhibited, combustible, cascade, ravine, gorge, frantically
Chapters 4–6: warbler, edible, depression, migration, snare, cicada
Chapters 7–10: poaching, talon, tether, provoke, trillium, carcass
Chapters 11–14: precaution, seized, inspiration, orphan, venison, hacksaw, ferocity, beady, cache
Chapters 15–18: sapling, ingenious, tallow, assured, community, lessened
Chapters 19–22: conscious, concoction, abundant, humanity, avalanche

warbler—
a small, brightly
colored songbird

Home Is Where The Heartwood Is

Sam Gribley makes his wilderness home in a hemlock tree. Work with your students to re-create a life-sized model of Sam's tree home using a refrigerator box. Cut an opening in the box front for a door. Then challenge students to locate descriptive references to Sam's home throughout the novel. Direct the students to use these descriptions to re-create Sam's tree using paint, construction paper, fabric scraps, and other art materials. Tape the top of the completed box closed and let your students use it throughout the year as a cozy reading corner.

A Boy's Best Friends

While Sam was in the wilderness, a falcon, a raccoon, and a weasel were his three best friends. Challenge each student to select one of these animals as the subject for further investigation. Direct each student to use reference materials to find out about the selected animal's appearance, diet, predators and/or prey, behavior, and other interesting facts. Then have each student write (or glue) a short informative report in the center of a large white paper plate. Along the perimeter of the plate, have the student glue small cutouts that illustrate facts from his report. After students share their reports with the class, display the eye-catching research plates in your room.

Getting The Scoop

Bando, the college professor, read newspaper reports to Sam about a wild boy living in the Catskill Mountains. Have each of your students imagine that she is a newspaper reporter assigned to interview that wild boy—Sam—and find out about his life in the wilderness. First direct each student to write several questions to ask Sam along with the responses she believes he would give. Then give each student a copy of page 127. Have the student use her interview questions and responses to write two newspaper articles about Sam on this reproducible. Post the completed copies of page 127 on a bulletin board labeled "Hot Off The Presses!"

The Raccoon

Barry Slate

Thanks For The Memories

A scrapbook is a book used to store a person's collection of pictures and mementos. After reading *My Side Of The Mountain,* challenge each of your students to create a scrapbook for Sam covering the time period he was in the wilderness. Have each student fold several sheets of 8 1/2" x 11" paper in half, punch two holes along the fold, and use twine to tie the pages together. Instruct each student to illustrate Sam's adventures and glue mementos made from scraps of construction paper in his scrapbook. Or, if your school is near a wooded area, take your students on an outdoor excursion to collect real mementos. Have each student securely glue each item and write an accompanying description of it in his scrapbook.

Survival Of The Fittest

Jean Craighead George successfully weaves actual facts about nature and wilderness survival throughout her fictional account of Sam Gribley's adventure in the Catskills. As you read the story, keep a running list on chart paper of these facts and the page numbers on which they are found. When you finish the story, divide your class into cooperative groups. Challenge each group to use the collected information to produce its own pamphlet on wilderness survival and nature. First instruct each group to select the ten facts it feels are most important to know to ensure wilderness survival. Then give the group a large sheet of construction paper on which to create its pamphlet. Put the completed pamphlets on display in your school's media center.

By George, I Think She's Got It!

Jean Craighead George has authored many other outstanding books for children. Continue your study of George by reading *On The Far Side Of The Mountain* (Puffin Books, 1991), the sequel to *My Side Of The Mountain.* Or select one of the following books:

The Summer Of The Falcon, illustrated by Jean C. George; published by HarperCollins Children's Books, 1993
Julie Of The Wolves, illustrated by Wendell Minor; HarperCollins Children's Books, 1994
The Wounded Wolf, illustrated by John Schoenherr; HarperCollins Children's Books, 1978
The Talking Earth; HarperCollins Children's Books, 1987
One Day In The Prairie, illustrated by Bob Marstall; HarperCollins Children's Books, 1986
Water Sky, illustrated by Jean C. George; HarperCollins Children's Books, 1989
Shark Beneath The Reef; HarperCollins Children's Books, 1991
The First Thanksgiving, illustrated by Thomas Locker; The Putnam Publishing Group, 1993

Name____________________

The New York Gazette

Poughkeepsie, New York | Vol. I, Issue 1 | May 1956

Interview With Boy Found Living In Catskill Wilderness

Sam Gribley, reported wild boy, is pictured here with his three animal friends.

How Boy Survived Severe Winter Weather In The Catskills

Gribley made his home in a hollowed-out hemlock tree to survive the harsh Catskill winter.

Note To The Teacher: Duplicate this page for each student. Use with “Getting The Scoop” on page 125.

Name ______________________________ *My Side Of The Mountain*

Critical thinking

The Gang's All Here!

At the end of the novel, Sam's family moves to the mountains to be with him. Imagine you are Sam. Write a journal entry describing how things have changed since your family's arrival.

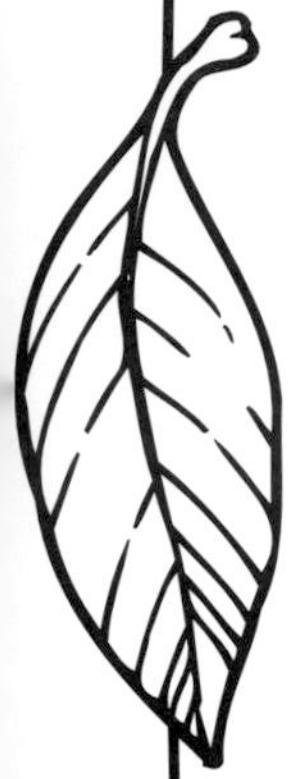

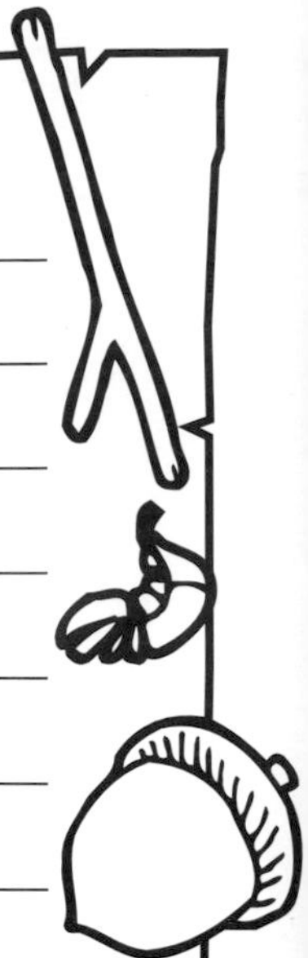

Sam

Name ______________________________ *My Side Of The Mountain*

Critical thinking

The Bare Necessities

Living in the wilderness alone would certainly be a challenging task! If you were going to run away and live in the Catskill Mountains like Sam, what five items would you take to help you survive? Below, list each item and the reason you selected it. Choose your items carefully!

ITEM	REASON
1.	
2.	
3.	
4.	
5.	

Note To The Teacher: Make two copies of this sheet for each student. Have each student fill out one copy before reading *My Side Of The Mountain* and the other after reading the novel. Challenge students to explain the differences between the two lists.

My Side Of The Mountain
Comprehension problems and solutions

What's The Problem (Or Solution)?

Sam Gribley encounters many problems while living in the wilderness alone. He solves many of these problems with the help of information he learned at the public library. Several of Sam's problems and solutions are listed below. Fill in the missing information based on what you have read in the story. Use the back if you need more space.

1. Problem: Sam needed food to keep himself alive until he reached his grandfather's mountain.
Solution: _____

2. Problem: _____
Solution: Miss Turner, the librarian, found the location of Gribley's farm in an old book on Delaware County.

3. Problem: Sam wondered if several different plants and insects were safe to eat.
Solution: _____

4. Problem: Sam wanted a home that could not be seen by hikers and campers.
Solution: _____

5. Problem: _____
Solution: Sam recalled that the Indians made dugout canoes with fire. So he hollowed out a hemlock tree in the same manner.

6. Problem: Sam wanted an animal to help him hunt food.
Solution: _____

7. Problem: Sam wanted salt to flavor the wild food he was eating.
Solution: _____

8. Problem: _____

9. Problem: Sam realized that his tree house would be cold if he did not find a way to heat it.
Solution: _____

10. Problem: Sam noticed that Frightful, his trained falcon, was sick.
Solution: _____

Solution: Sam made a deerskin suit using a bone needle and his old pair of city pants.

Bonus Box: On the back of this sheet, list three problems you have faced along with a description of how you solved each problem.

©1998 The Education Center, Inc. • *The Best Of The Mailbox® Literature • Intermediate* • TEC1464 • Key page 160

129

Note To The Teacher: Use this reproducible after students have read the first 15 chapters.

The House Of Dies Drear

A Spellbinding Mystery
by Virginia Hamilton

The huge, isolated mansion of white abolitionist Dies Drear was a former Underground Railroad station. Now it's home to 13-year-old Thomas Small and his family. Is it really haunted by slaves who were once housed there? And why are all these frightening things happening only hours after the Smalls arrive? Use the following literature activities and reproducibles to extend the reading of this edge-of-your-seat mystery about a black family caught in a web of suspense and danger.

by Loraine Moore

For Rent: A Most Unusual House

For the past 100 years, the house of Dies Drear hasn't been lived in for more than three months at a time—a challenge even the best real-estate agent might run from! For a fun creative-writing activity, collect a variety of real-estate ads from newspapers and local real-estate agencies. Have small groups of students study the ads. Discuss the characteristics of the house of Dies Drear (huge size, hidden passages and tunnels, steeped in history, etc.) and how those qualities could be seen as positives by the right customer. Then have each group design a flyer to convince prospective renters to give the house of Dies Drear a try! Post the flyers on a bulletin board entitled "For Rent: The House Of Dies Drear."

Student Detectives

As students read this suspenseful novel, they'll encounter more questions than answers. Well, that's the lot of a good detective! Let your students become regular gumshoes while they practice their critical-thinking skills. Cut a supply of duplicating paper in half so that each student has about ten pages. Have each student staple his pages inside a folded sheet of construction paper to make a clue book. After your students read a chapter (or you read a chapter aloud), write the critical-thinking question listed below on the board. Have students copy the question at the top of a page, then answer it either individually or after discussing it with a partner or small group. As students progress through the book, let them go back and revise their answers using clues from the book.

Critical-Thinking Questions To Answer After Chapter...

1—Why do you think there aren't any complete plans for the house?
2—Why do you think Mr. Small insisted that Thomas talk to no one about the foundation's report on the house or the legend of the three slaves?
3—Why do you think the Smalls' furniture had already been arranged for them?
4—What do you think Mac Darrow meant when he told Thomas, "But I suspect you'll be needing me later"?
5—What, if anything, do you think Mr. Small is keeping from Thomas?
6—What do you think Mr. Pluto meant when he shouted, "I have found it before you, and you ought to see it!"
7—Why do you think Mr. Small was looking so strangely at Mr. Pluto?
8—What do you think is haunting Mr. Pluto?
9—What or who left the triangles in the Smalls' house and Mr. Small's office?
10—Why do you think Mr. Darrow and his sons came to church that Sunday?
11—Why do you think the Darrows have something in for Pluto, like Carr said?
12—Who do you think vandalized the Smalls' kitchen?
13—What do you think Thomas and his dad saw when the wall slid open?
14—Who do you think is the "other" Mr. Pluto?
15—What do you think might be Mayhew's plan for the Darrows?
16—What secret about Mr. Pluto, Mayhew, and the Darrows do you think Mr. Small knows about?
17—How do you think Mayhew plans to scare the Darrows?

There's History In This Mystery!

In her novel, Hamilton weaves information about the Underground Railroad, the hardships of the slaves who "traveled" on it, and the work of abolitionists who staffed it. The theme of the importance of history is even personified in old Mr. Pluto, who passionately tries to preserve the history of Dies Drear and the slaves he helped escape to freedom.

Use this fascinating novel as a springboard to a study of the Underground Railroad and the time period in which it flourished. Have students study the lives of actual abolitionists and "conductors" on the Underground Railroad (see the list that follows). Read aloud excerpts from the following books to give students additional background information about slavery, the abolitionist movement, and the Underground Railroad:

Books:
- *Now Is Your Time! The African-American Struggle For Freedom* by Walter Dean Myers (HarperCollins): gives historical accounts taken from actual documents written by and about slaves.
- *Many Thousand Gone: African Americans From Slavery To Freedom* by Virginia Hamilton (Alfred A. Knopf, Inc.): draws on actual slave narratives.
- *Sojourner Truth: Ain't I A Woman?* by Patricia McKissack and Fredrick McKissack (Scholastic Inc.): a highly acclaimed biography about one of the most famous black abolitionists.
- *Underground Man* by Milton Meltzer (Harcourt Brace Jovanovich): tells the story of a white abolitionist who risks his life to rescue slaves from Kentucky.

Abolitionists:

James G. Birney	John Brown	Sojourner Truth
Frederick Douglass	William Lloyd Garrison	Elijah Parish Lovejoy
James Russell Lowell	Lucretia Mott	Alexander M. Ross
Elizabeth Cady Stanton	Harriet Beecher Stowe	Levi Coffin
Harriet Tubman		John Greenleaf Whittier

Live From The House Of Dies Drear

A lot of creepy things have been going on at the house of Dies Drear—just what a hungry news reporter likes to hear! Culminate the reading of this mystery classic by having students write and produce their own television news program. To prepare students for this activity, videotape suitable television interviews for the class to view and discuss. Next divide the class into pairs. Assign a character from the book to each pair: Thomas, Mr. Small, Mrs. Small, Mr. Pluto, Pesty, Mayhew, Mac Darrow, or one of the three Darrow brothers who were tricked. Have each pair write a five- to ten-question interview between a reporter and its character. Remind students of the following pointers about interviewing:

- Questions should be written to match the sequence of events in the book.
- Questions should be short and general so that the person being interviewed does most of the talking.
- Include questions that ask for the character's feelings and opinions.

Once students have written their interview questions and the character's answers, have each pair decide which partner will take the role of the reporter and which will be the character. Provide class time for students to practice their interviews. On the performance day, encourage students to come dressed in suitable costumes. Videotape the interviews; then watch the tape with students over a snack of hot popcorn.

The Black Trunk

At the end of the book, Thomas notices a black trunk hanging from the ceiling in the cavern. He decides to let the trunk remain a mystery—at least for now. Tickle your students' imaginations by asking them to think about what might be in the trunk. What would happen if the trunk fell? Tell students you want each of them to write a new mystery for Thomas and Pesty that starts when the trunk falls. Since mystery can be a difficult genre for young writers, help them get started by having each child divide a large piece of paper into thirds. Have the student label the tops of the three sections "Characters," "Setting," and "Plot"; then have her fill in the sections with information for her story. In the Plot section, encourage students to develop a problem the characters face and a solution to the problem. Once students have developed these plans, have each child write a short sequel to *The House Of Dies Drear.*

For students eager for a real sequel, never fear! Introduce them to *The Mystery Of Drear House* by Virginia Hamilton, which continues the story of the Small family and their life in Drear House.

When Thomas first moved into the house of Dies Drear,

Thomas was really scared when _____

Thomas was surprised when

In the end, Thomas _____

Glimpses Info

The House Of Dies Drear

Name: _____

Draw a picture of what you think is inside the black trunk.

How To Use This Page: Duplicate this sheet on white construction paper for each student. To make a picture flip book, have the student cut along the dotted lines. Then have him fold the page lengthwise along the longer solid line so that the writing is on the outside. Next have him fold the paper in half along the shorter solid line to form a booklet. Have the student open the booklet and finish each sentence; then have him lift the flap on which he's written and draw a picture to go with his writing. Finally have the student draw a picture on the back of his booklet as directed.

©1998 The Education Center, Inc. • *The Best Of* The Mailbox® *Literature* • *Intermediate* • TEC1464

A Chain Of Events

Events in a story are often related in a chain of causes and effects. An event that leads to other events is a *cause*. What happens as a result of the cause is its *effect*. The following questions can help you to identify whether a statement is a cause or an effect:

To find a cause, ask: "Why did it happen?"
To find an effect, ask: "What happened as a result?"

A single event can lead to many different effects. Fill in the blanks in the chart with what you think are the most important causes or effects.

Cause	Effect
1.	The house of Dies Drear has basically been empty for the past 100 years.
Someone sets up all the furniture in the house before the Small family arrives.	2.
3.	Thomas is trapped inside the kitchen wall.
4.	Thomas thinks Mr. Pluto is a devil.
Someone sneaks into the house through a secret passage while the Smalls sleep.	5.
6.	Thomas and his father find the hidden cavern of treasures.
7.	Mr. Pluto becomes terrified of the Darrows.
8.	Mayhew dresses up like his father.
Thomas, Mayhew, Mr. Pluto, and Mr. Small dress up like ghosts.	9.
Mr. Small decides to inventory the treasures in the cavern before telling anyone about it.	10.

Bonus: If Thomas and Mr. Small had never discovered the cavern, the mystery of Dies Drear's treasures would have remained a mystery. Pretend that Mr. Small has finished cataloging the treasures in the cavern. The foundation has asked him to hold a press conference to inform the public about the mystery of Dies Drear's treasures. On the back of this page, write the announcement that Mr. Small will make.

Chapter 1	**Chapter 2**	**Chapter 3**	**Chapter 4**	**Chapter 5**
dismal	relic	eaves	serene	varicolored
calamity	eccentric	quatrefoil	slimy	miniature
veranda	plunder	fertile	forlorn	crestfallen
sinister	caretaker	limestone	paralyze	tamper
desolation	agile	opaque	frantically	meander

Spelling At The House Of Dies Drear

Choose ___ words from *The House Of Dies Drear* for this week's spelling list. Circle the words you've chosen; then list them on the back of this page. Complete ____ of the activities listed below for homework this week.

Activities:

- Type your spelling words using our class computer.
- Write your words in *reverse* alphabetical order. Example: zebra, yellow, xylophone,…
- Make a set of flash cards for studying your words.
- Write newspaper headlines using your words.
- Estimate how much time it would take for you to copy your spelling list; then have a friend time you while you write each word one time. How close was your estimate to the actual time?
- Use the following code, a red marker, and a blue marker to write your spelling words.
  Code: *red* = vowels; *blue* = consonants.
- Draw or trace a simple shape, like a heart. Fill it in with your spelling words. Use colorful markers if you'd like.

★ ★ ★ ★ ★ ★ ★ ★ ★ ★ ★ ★ ★ ★ ★

Note To The Teacher: Have each student create his own personalized spelling list by choosing words from this page. Before duplicating the page, fill in the number of words and activities you want students to complete for homework during the week. If desired, pair students at the end of the week and have them test each other on the meanings and/or spellings of their words.

Chapter 6
ancient
eerie
jowls
emerald
massive

Chapter 8
superstitious
cubicle
stealthily
ornate
doorjamb

Chapter 10
segregated
refuge
congregation
pulpit
hostility

Chapter 13
ambush
sconce
falcon
recoil
forge

Chapter 7
threshold
cordial
spasm
specter
agitated

Chapter 9
hypotenuse
intruder
confide
misshapen
bellows

Chapter 11
aloofness
garret
musty
vicious
vandalism

Chapter 12
expanse
sprawling
comical
dread
delicately

Chapter 14
sentinel
cavern
tapestry
ledger
legacy

Chapter 15	**Chapter 16**	**Chapter 17**	**Chapter 18**	**Chapter 19**
grimly	anguish	elaborate	phosphorous	independent
obsessed	reprimand	shroud	gossamer	vaulted
fanatical	corridor	premonition	flimsy	intricate
heritage	hasty	squatter	alibi	inventory
mortal	lever	ancestor	malice	bulged

Thematic Booklists

Looking for the best books to enrich a favorite theme, a novel way to introduce areas of study, or a "sss-sensational" book for reading aloud? Then turn the page for books to excite your youngsters all year long!

Getting A Handle On History
Historical Fiction That Brings The Past To Life

History, the great teacher, mixes with fiction in the unforgettable novels recommended on the following pages. Through a variety of characters and story lines, the authors of these books bring history to life in a way that memorizing dates and facts could never accomplish. So sit back and prepare for an exciting journey to the past, where nearly everything is different—the communication, the travel, the dress. The only things that remain unchanged are the people and the tests of moral courage that they face.

reviewed by Deborah Zink Roffino

This Time, Tempe Wick?
written by Patricia Lee Gauch and illustrated by Margot Tomes
published by G. P. Putnam's Sons, 1992

The hills around eastern Pennsylvania become a makeshift encampment for Revolutionary War soldiers in 1779. Helping the soldiers is no problem for fiery Temperance Wick. She has a passion for her nation, as well as for a good cause. But when mutiny breaks out among the troops, Tempe must teach two wayward soldiers a few lessons in morality. Peppered with whimsical sketches, this account is based on both legend and fact.

By The Dawn's Early Light:
The Story Of The Star-Spangled Banner
written by Steven Kroll and illustrated by Dan Andreasen
published by Scholastic Inc., 1994

Experience the turmoil of three Americans held prisoner on British ships in the harbor next to Fort McHenry as they witness the Battle of Baltimore during the War of 1812. With researched details and exquisite full-page paintings, Steven Kroll offers this exciting narration of the moments that inspired lawyer Francis Scott Key to write "The Star-Spangled Banner."

Once On This Island
written by Gloria Whelan
published by HarperCollins Children's Books, 1995

This exciting novel takes place in 1812 on Mackinac Island in the Great Lakes. The war with Great Britain is tearing 12-year-old Mary O'Shea's family apart. News of the war travels slowly to the island's close-knit community of Irish, French, and Indian settlers. Tense and dramatic, poignant yet instructional, this story is told in the first person and offers a unique glimpse into the difficult decisions of loyalty and allegiance that arise during times of war.

The Captive
written by Joyce Hansen
published by Scholastic Inc., 1994

Packed with action and adventure, this superbly written story of an African prince taken captive holds lessons from history applicable today. The prince, Kofi, tells his story in first person. Through his moving narration, readers see African villages and family structure, the capture and transport of slaves, and the actions of both cruel and kind characters. Kofi is an unforgettable boy who provides a unique perspective for the readers of this fine novel.

On Winter's Wind
written by Patricia Hermes
published by Little, Brown And Company; 1995

This is the tender story of a family in New England just prior to the outbreak of the Civil War. Loyalties in the community are divided on the slavery issue, and tension rules every conversation. Genevieve's father has been gone for three years, having left by ship to secure his fortune. In addition, her mother is not well, and it is up to Gen alone to keep the family out of poverty. She must make a choice between turning in a runaway slave for the bounty or passing him to the Quaker station on the Underground Railroad.

Bull Run
written by Paul Fleischman and illustrated by David Frampton
published by HarperCollins Children's Books, 1994

Linked by time and the battle at Bull Run, this collection of fictional monologues illustrates how individuals' lives were forever altered by the Civil War. Together the eight accounts of Southerners and the eight accounts of Northerners tell a story of pain, loyalty, and disillusionment. This memorable collection teaches youngsters to approach the Civil War knowing that there are more than two sides to a story; in fact, there are as many different accounts as there are witnesses.

Jimmy Spoon And The Pony Express
written by Kristiana Gregory
published by Scholastic Inc., 1994

They covered 50 miles a day, and the work was so dangerous that the employees of choice for the Pony Express were orphans. This is the true story of the famed mail service that ran from St. Joseph, Missouri, to Carson City, Nevada. The factual account of the mail service is woven through the adventures of the fictional character Jimmy Spoon, an adventurous boy whose chronicles began in *The Legend of Jimmy Spoon*.

Flowers On The Wall
written and illustrated by Miriam Nerlove
published by Margaret K. McElderry Books, 1996

When examining the effects of the Holocaust, this lengthy picture book makes a perfect addition for the reluctant reader. The story is centered around Rachel, an eight-year-old Jewish girl living in Warsaw, Poland, in 1938. The story's rich text and somber watercolors paint a moving, heart-breaking story of a family's sacrifices, fear, and pain during this troubling period of history.

Molly Donnelly
written by Jean Thesman
published by Avon Books, 1994

Molly Donnelly's life changes dramatically with the bombing of Pearl Harbor. Her family is forced to ration, her mother must join the workforce, and Molly is left with all the chores and the responsibility of caring for her younger brother. But it is even more difficult for Molly to deal with the internment of her best friend, a Japanese-American. Molly demonstrates independence and strength as she learns to cope with the war, its prejudices, and its aftermath.

Room For A Stranger
written by Ann Turnbull
published by Candlewick Press, 1996

Set in England in 1941, this sequel to *No Friend Of Mine* focuses on the youngest Dyer, Doreen, and an evacuee, Rhoda, who comes to live with the Dyer family. Because the war has taken her father, devastated her home-land, and changed the direction of her life forever, Doreen doesn't take well to further upheaval—like sharing her room with Rhoda. The road to friend-ship for the two is complicated by the stress of the war and distrust.

Hiroshima
written by Lawrence Yep
published by Scholastic Inc., 1995

This spellbinding account by an award-winning author blends fact and fiction to detail the bombing of Hiroshima, Japan, during World War II. It is the story of 12-year-old Sachi—a witness to the arrival of the B-29 carrying the atomic bomb—who is seriously scarred and burned during the attack.

Other Recommended Titles

The Second Mrs. Giaconda
written by E. L. Konigsburg
published by Simon & Schuster Children's Books, 1978

Nettie's Trip South
written by Ann Turner
published by Simon & Schuster Children's Books, 1987

Thunder On The Tennessee
written by G. Clifton Wisler
published by Puffin Books, 1995

Dragon's Gate
written by Laurence Yep
published by HarperCollins Children's Books, 1995

Morning Girl
written by Michael Dorris
published by Hyperion Books For Children, 1992

Brooklyn Doesn't Rhyme
written by Joan W. Blos
published by Simon & Schuster Children's Books, 1994

Lyddie
written by Katherine Paterson
published by Puffin Books, 1992

Risk n' Roses
written by Jan Slepian
published by Scholastic Inc., 1992

Stepping On The Cracks
written by Mary D. Hahn
published by Houghton Mifflin Company, 1991

Good-Bye, Billy Radish
written by Gloria Skurzynski
published by Simon & Schuster Children's Books, 1992

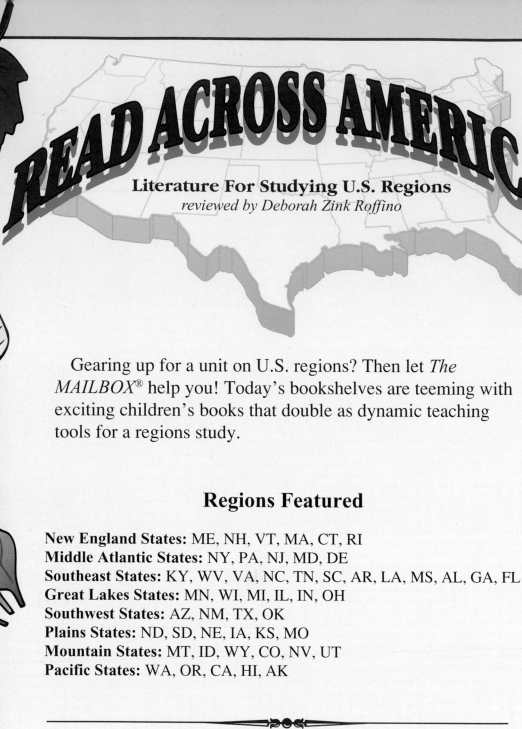

READ ACROSS AMERICA

Literature For Studying U.S. Regions
reviewed by Deborah Zink Roffino

Gearing up for a unit on U.S. regions? Then let *The MAILBOX®* help you! Today's bookshelves are teeming with exciting children's books that double as dynamic teaching tools for a regions study.

Regions Featured

New England States: ME, NH, VT, MA, CT, RI
Middle Atlantic States: NY, PA, NJ, MD, DE
Southeast States: KY, WV, VA, NC, TN, SC, AR, LA, MS, AL, GA, FL
Great Lakes States: MN, WI, MI, IL, IN, OH
Southwest States: AZ, NM, TX, OK
Plains States: ND, SD, NE, IA, KS, MO
Mountain States: MT, ID, WY, CO, NV, UT
Pacific States: WA, OR, CA, HI, AK

How To Use These Books

If you base your U.S. regions unit on cooperative group work, give each group the books suggested for the region it is studying; then have the group use the books to design and complete projects about the region. Have students read and compare books about the same region. Or challenge them to use some of the easier titles as models for writing their own region books. However you decide to use these outstanding titles, you can be sure that they'll take your students on an unforgettable journey across the USA.

MILK
one quart

New England States
(ME, NH, VT, MA, CT, RI)

Whaling Days
written by Carol Carrick and illustrated by David Frampton
Clarion Books, 1993

The history of whaling meshes with that of coastal New England hamlets. In this honest portrayal of a nearly vanished industry, the dramatic woodcuts slash over the pages, suggesting the power of the captured creatures and the strength of their captors. An extensive bibliography and index encourage further research and environmental studies.

A River Ran Wild
written and illustrated by Lynne Cherry
Harcourt Brace Jovanovich, 1992

Set in New England, this book is an environmental story of destruction and recovery. Man is the destroyer, but ultimately the hero, as history winds around the beautiful Nashua River in New Hampshire and Massachusetts. The river's survival intertwines with man's in this memorable picture book full of breathtaking vistas and powerful messages.

A New England Scrapbook: A Journey Through Poems, Prose, And Pictures
written and illustrated by Loretta Krupinski
HarperCollins Children's Books, 1994

The character and spirit of New England is lovingly communicated in this collection of paintings, prose, and poems about the region. From its old stone walls to its juicy cranberries and saltbox houses, New England comes vividly alive in the pages of this charming and informative book.

View From The Air: Charles Lindbergh's Earth And Sky
written by Reeve Lindbergh, with photos by Richard Brown
Viking Children's Books, 1992

Buckle your seat belt and climb into the cockpit! This fascinating book chronicles the last flights of Charles Lindbergh over rural New England. The beautiful color photographs are complemented by informative commentary—written by the famous aviator's daughter—about Lindbergh's views of the land.

Also Recommended:

Where The River Runs: A Portrait Of A Refugee Family *by Nancy Price Graff*
Little, Brown And Company; 1993

The times and trials of a Cambodian immigrant family are examined as they forge a new life near Boston.

The Storm *by Anne Rockwell*
Hyperion Books For Children, 1994

Salt-sprayed scenes of the rocky New England coastline illustrate this story of residents battening down for a nor'easter.

Ox-Cart Man *by Donald Hall*
Viking Children's Books, 1979

The story of a New England farm family of the 1800s, living a life that has been eliminated by today's advanced technology.

Middle Atlantic States
(NY, PA, NJ, MD, DE)

Voices Of The River:
Adventures On The Delaware
written by Jan Cheripko
Boyds Mills Press, 1994

From its source on the western slopes of the Catskills, the Delaware River flows south and forms the boundary between Pennsylvania and New York. This living geography book uses extensive text and breathtaking photographs to detail a canoe trip taken by the author and 14-year-old Matthew Smith along this magnificent waterway. This story of adventure offers a tremendous resource for any study of the Middle Atlantic region.

My New York
written and illustrated by Kathy Jakobsen
Little, Brown And Company; 1993

Capturing the bustle and excitement of a day in the city, this is no ordinary picture book. A few surprise pages unfold to sky-high-scrapers and reveal details that only the natives know: the locations of the flea market, the flower district, and Baby Watson's Cheesecake shop. This tempting excursion through the Big Apple glistens with lively folk art, maps, and postcard perspectives.

Hudson River:
An Adventure From The
Mountains To The Sea
written and photographed by Peter Lourie
Boyds Mills Press, 1992

Rock-studded streams, great green forests, rolling farmland, plunging cliffs, and white water—all are within view on this canoe trip down the Hudson River. Beginning at the river's source high in the Adirondacks and flowing to the southern tip of Manhattan, the 315-mile trip is recorded with clear, inviting photos. Surprises along the way include a castle and an amazing variety of landforms.

Amish Home
written and photographed by Raymond Bial
Houghton Mifflin Company, 1993

With intriguing detail, the staid simplicity of the Amish lifestyle is captured in this beautifully photographed narration. Originally a German Protestant group, the Amish live in 25 states, with large numbers in Pennsylvania. Readers get a rare, intimate look at the Amish, a religious people who remain as uncomplicated by technology as possible.

Also Recommended:

The Inside-Outside Book Of Washington, D.C. *by Roxie Munro*
Puffin Books, 1993

Familiar landmarks of our nation's capital are presented in fresh fashion for a real insider's look.

City Within A City: How Kids Live In New York's Chinatown *by Kathleen Krull*
Dutton Children's Books, 1994

Both traditional and contemporary lifestyles are explored in this look at one unique area of Manhattan.

The Folks In The Valley: A Pennsylvania Dutch ABC *by Jim Aylesworth*
HarperCollins Children's Books, 1992

A delightful alphabet book, illustrated in folk-art style, provides details about the people in a Pennsylvania Dutch settlement.

Southeast States
(KY, WV, VA, NC, TN, SC, AR, LA, MS, AL, GA, FL)

Appalachia:
The Voices Of Sleeping Birds
written by Cynthia Rylant and illustrated by Barry Moser
Harcourt Brace & Company, 1991

Nestled near the midpoint of the Appalachian Mountains, in West Virginia and Tennessee, lie countless, worn communities known as Appalachia. This book is a sensitive journey through this area of high, soft hills and deep, dark hollows. The expressive and evocative narration works with soft watercolors to beautifully portray the mists, glens, and guileless people of the mountains.

Marjory Stoneman Douglas,
Friend Of The Everglades
written by Tricia Andryszewski
The Millbrook Press, Inc.; 1994

This spirited biography reveals a pioneer whose vision and tenacity have made her an inspiration to all those with environmental concerns. From the 1920s until her 103rd birthday in 1993, Marjory Stoneman Douglas worked tirelessly to meet her goal of keeping the Everglades ecosystem, a national treasure, in an unsullied condition. This book includes in-depth explanations of the interdependence of the rivers, lakes, and wetlands.

Bridges To Change:
How Kids Live On A South Carolina Sea Island
written by Kathleen Krull, with photographs by David Hautzig
Dutton Children's Books, 1994

Gullah—a rare blend of English and West African languages—is the language and culture of St. Helena Island off the coast of South Carolina. Populated primarily by families of former slaves, the island was once separated from the mainland. Now bridges bring tourists, development, and change to the beautiful, pine-studded island. Splendid photography catches the isle, its people, and the natural terrain.

Everglades:
Buffalo Tiger And The River Of Grass
written and photographed by Peter Lourie
Boyds Mills Press, 1994

Photographer Lourie steers readers through the sharp-edged saw grass of the endangered Everglades. Along with his Native American guide, the author fights mosquitoes, avoids quicksand, and camps in a hammock of trees. The threatened ecology is highlighted by comparing early accounts and computer-enhanced maps. This book is an appeal to the young—stewards of the earth—to be cautious as they plan for the future.

Also Recommended:

Knoxville, Tennessee *by Nikki Giovanni*
Scholastic Inc., 1994
Impressionistic paintings and a lilting poem recall the author's summers in the South.

Seminole Diary: Remembrances Of A Slave *by Dolores Johnson*
Macmillan Publishing Company, Inc.; 1994
A young girl's diary divulges the close relationship between runaway slaves and the Seminole Indians in Florida.

Great Lakes States
(MN, WI, MI, IL, IN, OH)

In Coal Country
written by Judith Hendershot and illustrated by Thomas B. Allen
Alfred A. Knopf Books For Young Readers, 1987

In this short book, a young girl remembers her childhood in an Ohio coal-mining town in the 1930s. With subtlety and grace, the author and illustrator convey the poverty, hardship, and grime faced by the characters. Available in hardback and paperback.

The Mysterious Horseman:
An Adventure In Prairietown 1836
written by Kate Waters, with photographs by Marjory Dressler
Scholastic Inc., 1994

Illustrated with photos taken at the Conner Prairie Museum, a living history museum in Indiana, this is the account of a pioneer youngster who moves from a farm to a midwestern city. As 10-year-old Andrew adjusts to city life, readers learn about the food, crafts, trades, countryside, and history of this mid-American village. Actors from Conner Prairie Museum dramatize the story and lend authenticity.

County Fair
written and photographed by Raymond Bial
Houghton Mifflin Company, 1992

Toward the end of summer, folks in this part of the country gear up for an American tradition—the county fair. This book is a photographic peek behind the tents as the folks who pull together a county fair in Illinois prepare for opening day. Anticipation builds as the livestock pens, exhibitions, and midway rides materialize. A host of harvest colors draws in the reader—for lemonade, ice cream, and memories.

Johnny Appleseed And The Planting Of The West
written by Gina Ingoglia and illustrated by Charlie Shaw
Disney Press, 1992

John Chapman spent more than 40 years walking the hills of Pennsylvania and through Ohio, Indiana, and Illinois. Much of that land was forever changed due to his determination to seed the region with apple orchards. All sorts of gnarly growth, grassy pastures, rocky springs, and hilltop plateaus are encountered in this story, giving the reader a clear picture of the terrain.

Also Recommended:

Shannon: An Ojibway Dancer *by Sandra King*
Lerner Publications Company, 1993

A 13-year-old Ojibway girl from Minneapolis shares her preparations for a powwow at the Mille Lacs Reservation in central Minnesota.

If You Grew Up With Abraham Lincoln *by Ann McGovern*
Scholastic Inc., 1992

This paperback book offers rich details of frontier country, values, education, and folks in Indiana and Illinois a century and a half ago.

Southwest States
(AZ, NM, TX, OK)

The Armadillo From Amarillo
written and illustrated by Lynne Cherry
Gulliver Green® Books/Harcourt Brace & Company, 1994

For an excellent picture book of Texas geography and history, this delightful tale can't be beat. A wandering armadillo visits powdery fields of bluebonnets, a towering observation deck in San Antonio, and everything in between as he traverses the Lone Star State.

Cherokee Summer
written by Diane Hoyt-Goldsmith and photographed by Lawrence Migdale
Holiday House, Inc.; 1993

Reflecting a love of her heritage and a tremendous respect for the land, a young Cherokee Indian in Oklahoma explains the ways that her people mix tradition with progress. Folkloric tales, recipes, dances, and a smattering of Cherokee words from the syllabary of Sequoyah fill the pages of this tenderly photographed book.

This Place Is Dry
written by Vicki Cobb and illustrated by Barbara Lavallee
Walker Publishing Company, Inc.; 1989

Part of the Imagine Living Here series, this book explores life in the Sonoran Desert in Arizona. Cheerful illustrations support text that brims with fascinating facts about desert wildlife and how these life-forms have adapted to live in desert conditions.

Also Recommended:

Rio Grande Stories by Carolyn Meyer
Gulliver Books®/Harcourt Brace & Company, 1994

This collection of short stories applauds the diverse cultures and people of New Mexico.

Kinaaldá: A Navajo Girl Grows Up by Monty Roessel
Lerner Publications Company, 1993

A Navajo teen living in New Mexico runs the Kinaaldá, a traditional coming-of-age race for young girls.

Susanna Of The Alamo: A True Story by John Jakes
Gulliver Books®/Harcourt Brace & Company, 1990

The raw determination of a handful of brave, renegade Texans is captured in this historical picture book.

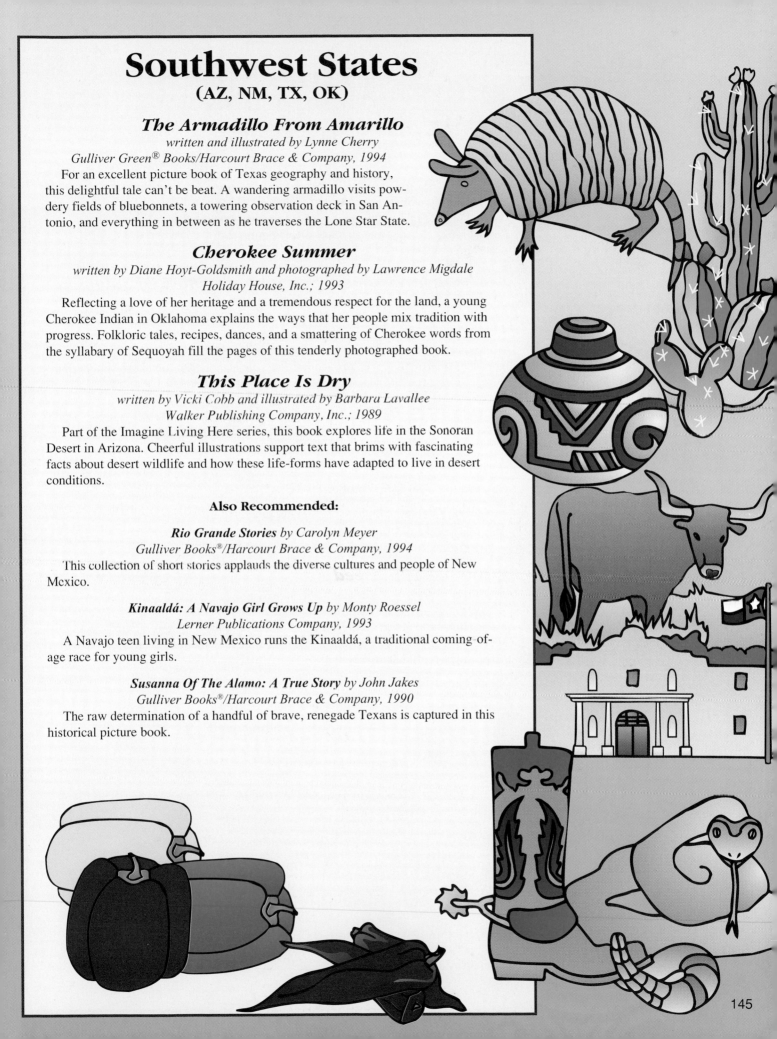

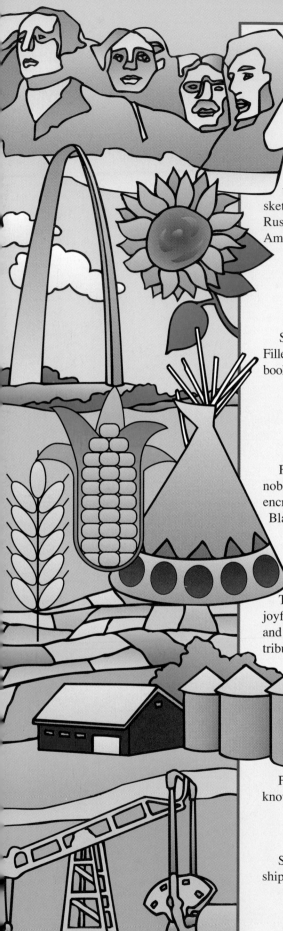

Plains States
(ND, SD, NE, IA, KS, MO)

An Indian Winter
written by Russell Freedman and illustrated by Karl Bodmer
Holiday House, Inc.; 1992

Follow the true, arresting adventures of a German prince and a Swiss painter as they travel the interior of North America in 1833. Their diaries, paintings, and sketches—lost to the public until 1962—are adeptly integrated by Newbery medalist Russell Freedman to create an unparalleled portrayal of the Dakotas and their Native American residents. A superior book for better readers.

Prairie Visions: The Life And Times Of Solomon Butcher
written by Pam Conrad with photographs by Solomon Butcher
HarperCollins Children's Books, 1991

Step back in time through the photos taken by a pioneer dreamer named Solomon Butcher. Filled with tales of the pioneer era and Butcher's life in turn-of-the-century Nebraska, this book captures the spirit and beauty of the prairie in a personal, evocative manner.

Tonweya And The Eagles And Other Lakota Indian Tales
retold by Rosebud Yellow Robe and illustrated by Jerry Pinkney
The Dial Press, 1979

From the northern Great Plains come these misty, unforgettable stories that honor the noble heritage of the Lakota Indian nation. These nomadic buffalo hunters resisted the encroachment of new cultures and carefully preserved their ways through oral tradition. Black-and-white drawings enhance this beautiful edition.

Heartland
written by Diane Siebert and illustrated by Wendell Minor
Thomas Y. Crowell Junior Books, 1989

Thumb through the pages of this stunning picture book and you'll be caught up in a joyful celebration of the Midwest. Patchwork-quilt fields of green and gold, giant mills and stockyards, the power of nature, and the fortitude of the farmer are applauded in this tribute to the heartland of America.

Also Recommended:

Corn Belt Harvest *by Raymond Bial*
Houghton Mifflin Company, 1991

Full-color photographs and easy-to-understand text introduce readers to the region known as the Corn Belt.

Summer And Shiner *by Nolan Carlson*
Hearth Publishing, 1992

Set in the Flint Hills of Kansas, this delightful story highlights the inseparable friendship of two boys and a pet raccoon named Shiner.

The American Family Farm *by Joan Anderson*
Harcourt Brace Jovanovich, 1997

Three families that work the land—including one from Iowa—are detailed in this photo-essay about life in rural America.

Mountain States
(MT, ID, WY, CO, NV, UT)

The Ancient Cliff Dwellers Of Mesa Verde
written by Caroline Arnold and photographed by Richard Hewett
Clarion Books, 1992

For a thousand years, the Anasazi Indians lived in a labyrinth of stone buildings on a plateau called Mesa Verde. Then they suddenly vanished, leaving behind baskets, tools, pottery, and empty rooms—abandoned and silent, except for the stories they tell to those who would listen. Using photographs of Mesa Verde National Park in Colorado, this fascinating book explores the history of the Anasazi tribe and its mysterious disappearance.

Yellowstone's Cycle Of Fire
written by Frank Staub
Carolrhoda Books, Inc.; 1993

The devastating summer of 1988 is chronicled in this fearsome account of fire fighting in America's most famous national park. Inspired photography highlights the region in dramatic fashion.

Powwow
written and photographed by George Ancona
Harcourt Brace Jovanovich, 1993

Through the gifted eye and lens of George Ancona comes a fiercely colorful picture of the yearly powwow of Native American tribes in Crow Agency, Montana. The engaging text explains the powwow in every detail as readers learn about the skills that are passed with pride from one generation to the next.

One Day In The Alpine Tundra
written by Jean Craighead George and illustrated by Walter Gaffney-Kessell
Thomas Y. Crowell Junior Books, 1984

In this slim volume, readers spend a summer day in the alpine tundra in the Teton Mountains of Wyoming. At times a no-man's-land and at other times a peaceful retreat, the tundra is home to an array of hardy wildlife that have adapted to the harsh conditions found there. This wonderful resource combines geography and science.

Also Recommended:

If You Traveled West In A Covered Wagon by Ellen Levine
Scholastic Inc., 1992

Across the widest parts of Wyoming and Idaho lay the toughest sections of the Oregon Trail. This paperback gives some of the best descriptions of that region that students can find.

Lewis And Clark: Explorers Of The American West by Stephen Kroll
Holiday House, Inc.; 1996

This information-packed picture book details the famous expedition through land that would one day be Montana, Idaho, and Wyoming.

Rocky Mountain Seasons: From Valley To Mountaintop by Diane L. Burns
Macmillan Publishing Company, Inc.; 1993

With stunning photographs and eloquent text, this picture book offers a close-up view of a magnificent mountain range and the effects the seasons have on it.

Pacific States
(WA, OR, CA, HI, AK)

Grizzlies
written by Lynn M. Stone
Carolrhoda Books, Inc.; 1993

Come to a windy Alaskan peninsula south of Anchorage and meet the local giants, the great brown grizzlies, in their enormous glory. With an impressive collection of close-up photographs, this nature book is a celebration of the majestic geography of the 50th state.

Voices From The Fields:
Children Of Migrant Farmworkers Tell Their Stories
written and photographed by S. Beth Atkin
Little, Brown And Company; 1993

Ten compelling stories told by children of Mexican-American migrant families paint an unforgettable picture of life in the Salinas Valley of California. From every perspective—the youth, the teens, the gang members, the honor students—these migrant children share their views on life's options.

Sea Otter Rescue: The Aftermath Of An Oil Spill
written and photographed by Roland Smith
Cobblehill Books, 1990

As oil from the *Exxon Valdez* spilled into the Prince William Sound in Alaska, animal conservationists rushed to help one of the most vulnerable of the threatened animals, the sea otter. In this compelling account, students will learn not only about the Alaskan coastline and its wildlife but also the danger an oil spill poses to the environment.

Townsend's Warbler
written by Paul Fleischman
HarperCollins Children's Books, 1992

Based on the journal of famed naturalist John Townsend, this engrossing chapter book traces the route he took on his transcontinental exploration in 1834. During an expedition beset by sandstorms, starvation, and Indian war parties, Townsend also encountered a black-and-yellow warbler unknown to scientists until then. This fascinating book contains revealing details about the northwestern United States.

Also Recommended:

The Great American Gold Rush by Rhoda Blumberg
Bradbury Press, 1989

Read about the mad dashes and perilous journeys gold seekers made across the unforgiving terrain of our great continent.

The Seasons And Someone by Virginia Kroll
Harcourt Brace & Company, 1994

With magnificent paintings, this picture book gives glimpses of the Alaskan landscape as seen through the eyes of a young Eskimo girl.

The Wonderful Towers Of Watts by Patricia Zelver
Tambourine Books/William Morrow & Company, Inc.; 1994

Climb magical towers built of junk in this true story of one man's quest to beautify a poor Los Angeles neighborhood.

Linking Up With Literature

Books About Recycling And Suggestions For Their Use

The Lorax
by Dr. Seuss

Who else but Dr. Seuss could weave a thought-provoking message into an enchanting tale? In this picture book, the selfish Once-ler decides to mass-produce "thneeds" (things we think we need), regardless of the effect on the environment. Though warned repeatedly by the Lorax, the Once-ler continues his greedy pursuits until nothing is left of the once-pristine land. Read *The Lorax* to students; then have the class brainstorm a list of present-day "thneeds" that hurt our environment. Have students suggest "thneed" alternatives that won't hurt the environment or create unnecessary waste. *Susan Myers—Gr. 4, Lockport Catholic Intermediate School, Lockport, NY*

Just A Dream
by Chris Van Allsburg

Sorting trash? Planting trees? Walter thinks it's all a waste of time—until the night he has a most unusual dream. After sharing this lovely picture book by Caldecott-winner Chris Van Allsburg, have students debate the question, "Can one person really make a difference?" At the end of the discussion, give each child a tagboard strip. Have the student copy and finish this sentence on his strip: "I can make a difference by _____." Post the strips on a bulletin board titled "A Healthy Earth Doesn't Have To Be Just A Dream."

Other books to use in your recycling studies:

Wastes by Christina G. Miller and Louise A. Berry
Recyclopedia: Games, Science Equipment, And Crafts From Recycled Materials by Robin Simons
Garbage by Karen O'Connor
Trash! by Charlotte Wilcox
Jack, The Seal And The Sea by Gerald Aschenbrenner
50 Simple Things You Can Do To Save The Earth by John Javna et al.
Worms Eat My Garbage by Mary Applehof

Where Does The Garbage Go?
by Paul Showers

Garbage—we're either making it or trying to get rid of it! In Paul Showers's informative book, readers learn what happens to dumped garbage and how it can be changed from an environmental menace to useful materials. Share this picture book with your students; then challenge each child to sift through his household's trash, find an item that could be reused, and bring it to school. (Caution students to avoid trash receptacles that contain glass or other dangerous materials. Bedroom trash cans are good sources of safe throwaways.) When everyone has brought in an item, hold a "Trash Bashers" forum during which each child shares his "throwaway" and presents a new use for it.

Mrs. Fish, Ape, And Me, The Dump Queen
by Norma Fox Mazer

It's not easy being raised by the manager of the town dump. Joyce is cruelly taunted by her classmates, who dub her "the Dump Queen." It takes the love of the school's "crazy" custodian to crack open the walls Joyce has built to keep out the hurt. As you read this novel together, have the class keep a running list of the way in which Joyce and her uncle follow the "three Rs": reduce, reuse, recycle. After finishing the book, have small groups discuss Joyce's situation at school; then have each group write a letter to Joyce suggesting ways she can deal with her classmates' teasing.

Make Mine A Mystery!
Spine-Tingling Whodunits Your Super Sleuths Will Love!

It's no mystery why mystery books are so popular. Teachers know that this genre sharpens powers of reasoning and deductive skills. Intermediate students plow through these books (often under the covers, with their flashlights on) for one reason: mysteries are just plain fun! The following excellent mysteries give students the thrill of solving a puzzle and one chill after another—what more could a reader ask for?

reviewed by Deborah Zink Roffino

Following are three sections: individual titles, serials, and novelty books. The books in each of these sections are listed in order from least difficult to more challenging.

Individual Titles

The Birthday Wish Mystery
Written by Faye Couch Reeves and Illustrated by Marilyn Mets
Little Rainbow®/Troll Associates, Inc.; 1994

Take easy text; short chapters; believable kids; and a strange, empty box that appears on the front doorstep—the result is this perfect first mystery book. Clues tumble across the pages, challenging readers to identify the enigmatic Annabelle Dupree before young Wynnie does. A host of characters send Wynnie on a series of searches. On the way she makes a friend, solves the puzzle, and learns just how much she is loved.

Mysteries Of Sherlock Holmes
Written by Sir Arthur Conan Doyle and Adapted by Judith Conaway
Bullseye Step Into Classics™/Random House, 1994

This reprinted classic is a terrific way for young readers to get hooked on one of the most famous detectives in literature. Three short mysteries—with an abundance of clipped, typical Holmes dialogue—offer the facts. Can you solve the mystery before Holmes? Large print and detailed black-and-white drawings make this edition less overwhelming than most versions.

The Seven Treasure Hunts
Written by Betsy Byars and Illustrated by Jennifer Barrett
HarperCollins Children's Books, 1991

Newbery-winner Betsy Byars appeals to reluctant readers in this hilarious chapter book. Two best friends spend every spare minute hiding treasure just for the sheer pleasure of unearthing it. When a delicious portion of the hoard truly disappears, the boys suspect sibling shenanigans and must apply all of their detective prowess to solve the mystery. Told engagingly in the first person, this book is peppered with clever black-and-white sketches that ably augment the story.

Marvelous Marvin And The Wolfman Mystery

Written by Bonnie Pryor and Illustrated by Melissa Sweet
Morrow Junior Books, 1994

Something *verrrry* weird is happening next door at Mr. Wolfe's house! The curious and suspicious Marvin Fremont begins some delightful detective work in this chapter book for medium-level readers. The believable plot draws on clues, secret cryptograms, and reasoning to build to a Halloween climax. Readers pleased with this adventure can check out the follow-up mystery, *Marvelous Marvin And The Pioneer Ghost* (1995), featuring the same crew of amateur sleuths.

The Bones In The Cliff

Written by James Stevenson
Greenwillow Books, 1995

Pete's abusive father is terrified of a big, mysterious stranger who smells like cigars. For moderately accomplished readers, this captivating story in first person carries the reader on a dramatic search for truth. On the way, the battered and weary Pete finds a lasting friendship and a better life.

Panther Glade

Written by Helen Cavanagh
Simon & Schuster Books For Young Readers, 1993

Mystery stalkers are lured by this sort of dark and menacing adventure in the wilderness. Young Bill accompanies his archaeologist aunt on a dig to a Calusa burial mound in Florida. His discovery of a small artifact believed to have great powers sends him on a solitary journey to learn the foundation of its legend. For stronger readers, this story features rich characters, heart-pounding tension, and a satisfying resolution.

The Missing 'Gator Of Gumbo Limbo: An Ecological Mystery

Written by Jean Craighead George
HarperCollins Children's Books, 1992

One of the first environmental writers for youngsters is still one of the best. Jean Craighead George lures more accomplished readers into the Gumbo Limbo section of the Everglades. When an official tries to do away with Dajun, an enormous alligator, Liza K. must find the missing 'gator with careful detective work and an ability to read environmental clues. It's botany, ecology, biology, and mystery all in one terrific book!

The Sluggers Club: A Sports Mystery
Written by Paul Robert Walker
Harcourt Brace Jovanovich, Publishers; 1993

Competent readers are rewarded in this baseball/detective novel with fully developed characters, more twists than a triple play, lessons on vicious prejudice, and a full-blown puzzler. Baseball aficionados will follow the Matt Christopher-style play-by-play better than the uninformed, but even nonfans can get hooked as equipment vanishes, questions multiply, and suspicious characters surface.

Super Serials For Super Sleuths

The Boxcar Children® Special #3:
The Mystery At Snowflake Inn
Created by Gertrude Chandler Warner and Illustrated by Charles Tang
Albert Whitman & Company, 1994

For those unfamiliar with this popular series, four children are found living alone in a boxcar and are taken in by their grandfather. The adventures the children encounter while learning to be a family provide the framework for the simple mysteries they solve. The text offers strong context clues for new vocabulary and mixes history lessons in the story line. Several books in the series—including this one about a puzzling holiday trip to an old-fashioned New England inn—end with several pages of puzzles, games, and recipes that reflect the plot.

The Kerry Hill Casecrackers #4:
The Case Of The Mysterious Codes
Written by Peggy Nicholson and John F. Warner
Lerner Publications Company, 1994

The mystery starts instantly with the arrival of coded messages and some ominous and unwelcome gifts. The Casecrackers—sharp, young detectives from New England—use logical deductions and powers of observation to get to the resolution of their cases. Like Nancy Drew and the Hardy Boys, these kids from Kerry Hill start to feel like old friends after one book. And, delightfully, there are four books in this fine new series.

Welcome Inn #3: The Skeleton Key
Written by E. L. Flood
Rainbow Bridge®/Troll Associates, Inc.; 1994

Don't be scared off by the cover images of haunted houses and grave digging; this is good, tense fun without any gore or supernatural villains. Plodding, old-fashioned detective work solves this mystery for moderately strong readers. Close calls, dark encounters, and foreboding disappearances engage the reader from page one to the satisfying and reasonable conclusion.

3.

4.17.5.11,
22.15.8, 3.6.19.11.13
13.21, 6.23, 14.2.9
7.1.9.

Novelty Books

Puzzle Island

devised, written, and illustrated by Paul Adshead
Child's Play (International) Ltd, 1995

For individual or group detective work, this creative puzzle/book challenges youngsters to read a diary, decipher the clues, make inferences, and then identify and help rescue an endangered species. Lush tropical paintings give this paperback the tone of a picture book. But don't be too quick to jump to conclusions; traces of evidence are hidden with great skill in the detailed jungle scenes. Amateur sleuths will compete to solve this fascinating mystery.

Whodunit: Science Solves The Crime

written by Steven Otfinoski and illustrated by Betsy Scheld
Scientific American Books For Young Readers/W. H. Freeman and Company, 1995

Ten fascinating chapters, each featuring a real criminal case, demonstrate the science of forensics. Dating back to the 1800s, the cases touch each new technology—including fingerprinting, DNA, tissue analysis, ballistics, and the detection of poison—that leads to resolution of a mysterious crime. Vibrant art provides an interruption of the text, making the information less intimidating and more storylike. This slim compendium offers an intriguing link between technology and mysteries, and between the science curriculum and reading.

More Marvelous Mysteries

The Disappearing Bike Shop
by Elvira Woodruff; Holiday House, Inc.; 1992

Spider Kane And The Mystery Under The May-Apple
by Mary Pope Osborne; Knopf Books For Young Readers, 1992

Skateboard Tough
by Matt Christopher; Little, Brown And Company; 1991

The Man Who Was Poe
by Avi; Avon Books, 1991

The View From The Cherry Tree
by Willo Davis Roberts; Aladdin/Macmillan Children's Book Group, 1994

The Court Of The Stone Children
by Eleanor Cameron; Puffin Books, 1990

SSS-Simply SSS-Sensational

Favorite Read-Aloud Ideas From Our Subscribers

When we asked our subscribers for their favorite read-aloud books and activities, we were sss-simply sss-swamped with sss-super sss-suggestions! Slithering through the next six pages are your teaching peers' read-aloud recommendations, accompanied by fun literature activities. Sss-so get ready to instill a love for reading in your sss-students!

Picture Books

Chrysanthemum

Written and Illustrated by Kevin Henkes
Published by Greenwillow Books

Chrysanthemum used to think her name was perfect—that is, until the first day of school when all the other mice laughed at her. After reading this charming book to my class, I have students research the origins and meanings of their names. Students are encouraged to talk with parents about how their names were chosen; then each child writes an acrostic using the letters of his name. Students are instructed to complete their acrostics with words and phrases that reflect the meanings of their names as well as their unique personalities and interests. This activity really helps my students feel special and "blossom"—just like Chrysanthemum!
Susan Hendrix—Gr. 5, Old Town Elementary, Round Rock, TX

Sam's Sandwich

Written and Illustrated by David Pelham
Published by Dutton Children's Books

In this delightful rhyming tale, Sam makes a sandwich for his sister. But this is no ordinary sandwich! Much to the delight of your listeners, Sam hides all manner of "creepy crawlies" in the sandwich. After reading this story to my class, I have each child fold a piece of paper in half, labeling one side BUGS and the other side ADJECTIVES. I give the students two minutes to brainstorm words for each section. Then I place a transparency showing a poem pattern on the overhead to help students write their own "buggy" poems. After the inspiration offered by *Sam's Sandwich* and the brainstorming session, my students produce some very "f-ant-astic" poetry!
Danielle Weisse Lewing—Gr. 5, Hastings Elementary, Crossett, AR

The Relatives Came

Written by Cynthia Rylant & Illustrated by Stephen Gammell
Published by Bradbury Press

What happens when a crowd of relatives descends on a family one summer day? Chaos, commotion—and a ton of love! After sharing this irresistible Caldecott Honor Book, my students and I discuss family reunions and get-togethers we've attended. Then each child chooses a favorite relative and writes an essay about him or her. I encourage students to use lots of descriptive words and to include reasons why the chosen relatives are their favorites. Finished essays can be bound in a class book entitled "Relatively Speaking"! *Wanda L. Mollett—Grades 5–7, Meade Memorial Elementary, Williamsport, KY*

Read-Alouds

The Z Was Zapped: A Play In Twenty-Six Acts

Written and Illustrated by Chris Van Allsburg
Published by Houghton Mifflin Company

This incredibly creative alphabet book really grabs my students' attention. Each right-hand page shows an unusual illustration of a letter (for example, an *N* riddled with nails or an *I* that is partially covered with icing). On the back of the illustration is a sentence explaining the picture (for example, "The N was Nailed and Nailed again.") After letting students guess what is happening to each letter, I have each child choose a letter and design his own page for the "second edition" of the book. Each child shows his finished illustration to the class; then the other students try to guess what is happening to that letter. What fun! *Shelley Higginbotham—Substitute Teacher, El Cajon, CA*

The True Story Of The Three Little Pigs

Written by Jon Scieszka & Illustrated by Lane Smith
Published by Viking Children's Books

After reading Jon Scieszka's humorous version of the famous fairy tale—told from the wolf's point of view—get ready for a courtroom drama even Perry Mason would be proud of! Assign students the roles of the three pigs, the wolf, lawyers, a judge, jurors, witnesses, and a bailiff. Have the wolf and his lawyers prepare to defend his case. Of course, the three pigs and their attorneys will want to do all they can to prove the wolf's guilt. At the end of the trial, have the jury decide which story is the true story of the three pigs—the traditional one or the account told by the wolf. This activity is a great way to introduce students to a unit on the judicial system. *Kelly A. Wong—Grs. K–6, Diamond Bar, CA*

Alexander And The Terrible, Horrible, No Good, Very Bad Day

Written by Judith Viorst & Illustrated by Ray Cruz
Published by Atheneum Books For Young Readers

Have you ever had one of those truly rotten days when absolutely nothing goes right and everything that could possibly go wrong does? Alexander is having one of those days, and kids of all ages (and adults, for that matter) will readily sympathize with this frustrated little boy. When my students and I are having one of those really awful days, I stop everything and read Viorst's hilarious book to my class; then we discuss the book and our day. I have each child draw a caricature of himself to illustrate what might make his day terrible, horrible, no good, and very bad. By the time we finish, we've all had a good laugh. *Virginia M. O'Connor—Gr. 5, St. Raphael School, Medford, MA*

The Araboolies Of Liberty Street

Written by Sam Swope & Illustrated by Barry Root
Published by Clarkson N. Potter, Inc.

When mean General Pinch orders the Araboolies to move because they're a bit different, the kids of Liberty Street join forces to save their unusual neighbors. After I share the book with students, we work together to turn the story into a play. We make simple Liberty Street "houses" by stapling white canvas onto wooden frames. On one side of each canvas set, students paint a house outline (to resemble the white houses at the beginning of the book). On the other side, students paint a wildly decorated house (similar to those found at the end of the story). During our performance, when the play reaches the climax, students simply turn the plain white houses around to reveal ones painted by the Liberty Street kids! *Katherine Maher, East Broad Street Elementary, Savannah, GA*

Novels

The Trumpet Of The Swan
Written by E. B. White & Illustrated by Edward Frascino
Published by HarperCollins Children's Books

E. B. White's enchanting story of Louis, a trumpeter swan born without a voice, is one of my all-time favorite read-alouds. Before reading this book to my students, I displayed a stuffed toy swan (actually a transformed stuffed Mother Goose). As we continued reading, students brought in or made models of items Louis gathers in his journeys. For example, my students strung a toy trumpet on yarn and draped it around Louis's neck. Later they added a small chalkboard and a gold medal. My students loved watching our display grow as we read the book. *C. B. Sellen—Library Director, Walter Hill School, Swedesboro, NJ*

Mary Poppins
Written by P. L. Travers
Published by Dell Publishing Company

Who doesn't love the most famous nanny in the world? While I'm reading this timeless fantasy, I hang an umbrella up-side-down from my ceiling. Inside the umbrella I place a set of activity cards based on the book. Once a week each child chooses an activity from the umbrella to complete. For example, a student might be asked to write a newspaper article titled "Mary Poppins: What I'm *Really* Like" or to draw a floor plan of the perfect house for Mary. With Mary Poppins, the possibilities are endless! *Sonya Franklin—Gr. 5, Ladonia Elementary, Phenix City, AL*

Charlotte's Web
Written by E. B. White & Illustrated by Garth Williams
Published by HarperCollins Children's Books

During or after reading this classic book, divide your class into three groups: newspaper, radio, and television. Choose one important event from the book, such as when the words "SOME PIG" appear on the web. Have each group prepare a news report that its form of media might produce. The newspaper reporters will soon learn that their audience relies only on print and pictures to receive the message. The radio announcers will find that they must develop certain techniques to present a clear message without the use of pictures. Even your television groups will discover disadvantages to videotaped news reporting. My students love giving their news presentations to other classes to sell them on reading the book for themselves. *Mary Rubino Kibbey, Athens Elementary, Athens, NY*

The Boxcar Children®
Written by Gertrude Chandler Warner
Published by Albert Whitman & Company

Orphaned by the death of their parents, four children are determined to evade the custody of their grandfather and survive on their own. But will the refuge of an abandoned boxcar shield the children from discovery? The children in this popular tale (first in a series of 19 books) refer to objects found near their boxcar as "treasures." To culminate reading, I plan a treasure hunt. First I gather a collection of inexpensive items mentioned in the book (for example, a package of beef jerky, a small broom, a pink cup, etc.). I wrap each item, making sure that I have one gift per student, and hide the packages. On the day of the hunt, students find their gifts; then we unwrap them and each child explains how his gift relates to the book. We end our hunt with a special "boxcar lunch" prepared by parent volunteers. *Cathy Woodward, McKinley School, Newton, KS*

Maniac Magee
Written by Jerry Spinelli
Published by Joy Street Books

This 1991 Newbery Medal winner is the story of a young boy who works to unite a town divided by racial prejudices. During reading, each of my students kept a private response journal in which he reacted to the events in the story. As a culminating activity, each child put himself in the place of Jeffrey "Maniac" Magee and wrote about whether he would have tried to unite the town. My students held passionate views about fighting prejudice, which led to a wonderful discussion of how to incorporate their ideas into our school and community. It was the most painless lesson on persuasive writing I've ever taught! *Deborah Calvert—Gr. 5, Landis Elementary, Alief, TX*

When Maniac unites the famous Cobble's Knot, he wins a prize that would excite any kid—one free, large pizza per week for a whole year! When your class finishes *Maniac Magee* or meets a difficult goal, reward students with a pizza-making session. Bring prepackaged dough, pizza sauce, and toppings. Then divide students into groups and let each team make its own pizza for lunch. Enjoy the pizza while you review favorite parts of *Maniac Magee. adapted from an idea by Sonya Franklin—Gr. 5*

Chocolate Fever

Written by Robert Kimmel Smith & Illustrated by Gioia Fiammenghi
Published by The Putnam Publishing Group

Henry Green is totally insane about chocolate, making him a prime candidate for the first case ever of chocolate fever. After reading this merry misadventure, I challenge each student to create his own one-of-a-kind disease. Students write descriptions of their diseases, including names, causes, freaky symptoms, and surefire cures. I also ask each child to include an illustration of someone who has been unfortunate enough to contract his curious malady. We bind all of our pages into a class "Medical 'Fictionary.' " *Anna Bordlee— Gr. 5, Boudreaux Elementary, Harvey, LA*

When we finished reading *Chocolate Fever,* my students published their own *Chocolate News,* a newspaper highlighting all of the new information we had learned about chocolate. We included articles that reviewed the book, gave the history of chocolate, explained how chocolate was made, shared favorite chocolate recipes, and much more. Final copies were distributed to all the chocolate lovers in our school—which included absolutely everyone! *Linden Snyder—K–6 Resource, Goldfield Elementary, Goldfield, IA*

Stinker From Space

Written by Pamela Service
Published by Juniper

When alien Tsynq Yr crashes his spaceship in midwestern America, mortally injuring his body, he must quickly locate another one to occupy. Unfortunately, the only available host happens to be a skunk! Pamela Service's side-splitting fantasy is a great way to get my students back in the groove after a long summer vacation. After finishing the book, we hold a "Stinker Day." Students wear black and white clothing (to resemble skunks) to school. Since the main character thought peanut butter was a wonderful delicacy, we make no-bake peanut butter cookies and eat peanut butter sandwiches. Finally we divide into research teams to uncover facts about skunks, converting our information into skunk booklets. *Becky French— Gr. 5, Overland Park Elementary, Kansas City, MO*

Freaky Friday

Written by Mary Rodgers
Published by HarperCollins Children's Books

Imagine the shock of 12-year-old Annabel Andrews when she awakens one Friday morning to discover that she's switched bodies with her mother! I begin reading this zany book to my students at the end of April, finishing it just before Mother's Day. To celebrate, my students invite their mothers to a Freaky Friday Mother's Day Party. At this party, children and moms come dressed as each other—always a hilarious sight to see! After the party, each child writes about what it would be like to switch places with a parent. My students and parents love this fun-filled activity and the book it's based on! *Camille Luce—Gr. 4, Boone Elementary, Alief, TX*

How To Eat Fried Worms

Written by Thomas Rockwell & Illustrated by Emily McCully
Published by Franklin Watts, Inc.

Billy's bet—to eat 15 worms in 15 days—is told in short, rollicking chapters in this all-time children's favorite. On the day I finish reading the book to my students, I give each child a supply of Gummy Worms®. While we enjoy the treat, students share their favorite parts of the book. For a writing extension, have each child write a paragraph describing his personal, as-painless-as-possible method for eating a worm. Another Gummy Worm, anyone? *Pat Fleming—Gr. 4, South Boulevard Elementary, Baton Rouge, LA*

Thanksgiving Treasure

Written by Gail Rock & Illustrated by Charles C. Gehm
Published by Alfred A. Knopf, Inc.

Inviting enemies to dinner—it was an idea that grabbed young Addie Mills's attention and hung on. Begin reading this touching book during the first week of November so that the follow-up activities can be completed before Thanksgiving vacation. After the book is finished, we have each child write an epilogue (written in first person, like the book), telling what happened to Addie after Mr. Rehnquist died and left his horse to her; then read author Rock's epilogue and compare it to the students' versions. It's a wonderful way to usher in the true spirit of Thanksgiving. *adapted from an idea by Kathleen Natzel—Gr. 5, Big Sky Elementary, Billings, MT*

Turn Homeward, Hannalee

Written by Patricia Beatty
Published by Morrow Junior Books

When it's time to study the Civil War, be sure to add this riveting novel to your plans! After being forced by Union soldiers to work against her will in a Yankee mill, 12-year-old Hannalee Reed vows to make her way back home to Georgia and the family she was forced to leave behind. While sharing the book, I have students compare the information given about the Civil War with the facts found in our textbooks. We also pretend to be soldiers or civilians involved in the war and write letters describing our experiences. *Sonya Franklin—Gr. 5, Ladonia Elementary, Phenix City, AL*

The View From The Cherry Tree

Written by Willo Davis Roberts
Published by Aladdin Paperbacks

When Rob, known for his tendency to exaggerate, witnesses a murder, only one person believes him—the murderer! While reading this tense murder mystery, my students discuss the suspects and their alibis. Each child then writes a prediction about who the murderer is. We tally the predictions on the chalkboard and make graphs to illustrate our data. Excitement builds as we progress toward the end of the book and the murderer is exposed! *Paula M. Gulley—Gr. 5, Duchesne Elementary, Florissant, MO*

The Great Gilly Hopkins

Written by Katherine Paterson
Published by HarperCollins Children's Books

Gilly is a bratty, angry child who makes life for her foster parents, the Trotters, more than a little interesting. After reading this sensitive novel to my students, we have a little fun by holding a "Melvin Trotter Ugly Tie Contest." I give each chid a tie pattern with instructions to design a flamboyant tie that Melvin (known for his ugly ties) would be sure to wear. The entries are posted in the classroom; then we invite another class that has read the book to visit and select the top three ties. This is a popular activity that ends the book on an upbeat note. *Nancy M. Newman—Gr. 5, Ocean Township Intermediate School, Ocean, NJ*

Hatchet

Written by Gary Paulsen
Published by Puffin Books

After sharing this thrilling tale of a young boy's survival in the Canadian wilderness, I planned a special Survival Day for my students. I pushed student desks into a semicircle and covered them with brown paper. Paper trees and pictures of wild animals mentioned in the book were taped to the desks to represent the wilderness. I placed a small table on top of a larger one and covered both with brown paper to represent Brian's rock shelter. I also placed a large, blue paper lake on the floor, adding real rocks around the shoreline.

The next day I greeted the children in the hallway and announced that we would be taking a plane into the Canadian wilderness. After discussing our flight plan, we logged the time of our departure and silently entered the room. Students were greeted by tape recordings of lapping waves and water birds. We spent the whole day in our environment completing a variety of book-related activities. For example, students created math problems about the animals in the wilderness, wrote "missing person" articles about Brian, and read favorite parts of the book while curled up in the rock shelter. *Suzanne Okas, Mineral Point Elementary, Mineral Point, WI*

A Wrinkle In Time

Written by Madeleine L'Engle
Published by Dell Publishing Company, Inc.

After reading this science fiction classic, each of my students selected a character on which to become an expert. On a designated day, I asked several students to sit at the front of the room. Some of the students dressed as their characters and others wore nametags. One child acted as the moderator and entertained questions from the floor. I was amazed at the thought-provoking questions and depth of characterizations displayed by my students. *Teresa Williams—Grs. 4–5, Silver Creek Elementary, Hope, British Columbia, Canada*

The Secret Garden
Written by Frances H. Burnett & Illustrated by Tasha Tudor
Published by HarperCollins Children's Books

After reading this celebrated novel about a spoiled orphan who finds new health and happiness on her guardian's estate, I used the book as a theme for our school's Open House. Students worked together to turn our room into the secret garden. For example, we hung green crepe-paper streamers from the top of our door to represent vines. Students drew, colored, and cut out life-sized pictures of the book's characters to post around the room. We even made a wheelchair for Colin by taping large cardboard wheels to a folding chair. Our project was a wonderful way to celebrate this terrific book and involve our parents in the fun! *Connie King—Media Aid, Deerlake Middle School, Tallahassee, FL*

I, Houdini: The Autobiography Of A Self-Educated Hamster
Written by Lynne Reid Banks & Illustrated by Terry Riley
Published by Doubleday & Company, Inc.

What kid wouldn't love a story about an escape-artist hamster named Houdini? Written from the hamster's point of view, this book offers the perfect opportunity to write first-person accounts. I have each of my students create his own "hamster diary" in which he writes about his experiences as a hamster. It's a super way to teach an important literary concept! *Laura M. Earp—Chapter I Reading, Indian Valley School, Radford, VA*

The Indian In The Cupboard
Written by Lynne Reid Banks & Illustrated by Brock Cole
Published by Avon Camelot Books

Omri is thrilled when his toy plastic Indian magically comes to life. But soon he learns that being in charge of a live person is no small responsibility! After reading this book to my class, I give each child his very own plastic Indian or cowboy figure. Students name their figures; then they write stories explaining how the figures came to life and describing adventures they shared with them. I also encourage students to illustrate their stories and design shadow-box "homes" for their little friends. This fun project leads naturally into a follow-up study of Native American cultures. *Nancy M. Grow—Gr. 5, Westchester School, Kirkwood, MO*

The Cay
Written by Theodore Taylor
Published by Doubleday & Co., Inc.

My students love this spellbinding tale of a young boy blinded and shipwrecked on a Caribbean island with an elderly black man. After reading it to your students, discuss 12-year-old Phillip's self-centeredness and prejudice toward old Timothy. Ask students to explain why they think Phillip refused Timothy's help. Then have each child write a personal essay about a time when he had to depend on someone else for help. While students are working on their essays, serve homemade banana bread (bananas were a staple food for the shipwrecked twosome) and play Caribbean music in the background. *adapted from ideas by Maxine Pincott—Gr. 4, Oliver Ellsworth School, Windsor, CT*

Little House In The Big Woods
Written by Laura Ingalls Wilder & Illustrated by Garth Williams
Published by HarperCollins Children's Books

To follow up reading of this favorite novel, I had a friend build a 6' x 4' wooden frame with two windows and a door. The students used their measurement skills to cut cardboard to use for the outer walls and roof of our "log cabin." After decorating the cardboard to resemble logs, students filled the cabin with pioneer items, such as a rocking chair, oil lamps, a butter churn, and home-canned foods. When we finished the book, we used the cabin as a reading center. *Debbie Clark, Newton Rayzor Elementary, Denton, TX*

I'm Going To Be Famous
Written by Tom Birdseye
Published by Yearling Books

This book about a boy who wants to be in the *Guinness Book Of World Records* is one of my all-time favorites. After we finish the book, I have each child cut out a magazine picture that illustrates a feat he would like to accomplish. We examine the format used in the record book; then each child types a world-record entry to accompany his picture. We bind the pictures and records together in a class book. *Kathy Bray—Gr. 4, West School, Carlinville, IL*

Answer Key

Page 41
1. *The Story Of Mankind*, 1922
2. *Maniac Magee*, 1991
3. *A Wrinkle In Time, A Gathering Of Days, A Visit To William Blake's Inn*
4. *Miss Hickory; Carry On, Mr. Bowditch; From The Mixed-Up Files Of Mrs. Basil E. Frankweiler; Mrs. Frisby And The Rats Of NIMH; Dear Mr. Henshaw*
5. *Smoky, The Cow Horse; Amos Fortune; Free Man; Carry On, Mr. Bowditch; It's Like This, Cat; I, Juan de Pareja; M. C. Higgins, The Great; Roll Of Thunder, Hear My Cry; Sarah, Plain And Tall*
6. *It's Like This, Cat; A Visit To William Blake's Inn; Dicey's Song*
7. *The Story Of Mankind, The Voyages Of Doctor Dolittle, The Dark Frigate, The Trumpeter Of Krakow, The Cat Who Went To Heaven, The White Stag, The Matchlock Gun, The Twenty-One Balloons, The Door In The Wall, The Wheel On The School, The Witch Of Blackbird Pond, The Bronze Bow, The High King, The Summer Of The Swans, The Slave Dancer, The Grey King, The Westing Game, The Hero And The Crown, The Whipping Boy*
8. *Waterless Mountain, Invincible Louisa, Caddie Woodlawn, Roller Skates, Thimble Summer, Daniel Boone, Johnny Tremain, Rabbit Hill, Strawberry Girl, Miss Hickory, Ginger Pye, Onion John, Dicey's Song, Maniac Magee*
9. *The Dark Frigate, The White Stag, Call It Courage, The Matchlock Gun, The Twenty-One Balloons, …And Now Miguel, Rifles For Watie, The Bronze Bow, The High King, The Slave Dancer, The Grey King, Bridge To Terabithia, The Westing Game, Dear Mr. Henshaw, The Whipping Boy, Lincoln: A Photobiography, Number The Stars*

Page 111
1. Turtle Wexler
2. Berthe Erica Crow
3. Judge J. J. Ford
4. Sydelle Poulaski
5. Otis Amber
6. Angela Wexler
7. Grace Wexler
8. Sander McSouthers
Hidden message: He is not dead.

Page 129
Problem
2. Sam needed to find out where his grandfather's land was located.
5. Sam was having a hard time carving out the inside of the tree he had selected to be his home.
8. Sam needed warm, durable clothing.
Solution
1. Sam made a fishing tool from twigs and string, gathered grubs from a rotten log, and caught fish.
3. Sam watched what the birds and animals were eating to see what plants and insects were edible.
4. Sam made a home in a hemlock tree trunk.
6. Sam captured and trained a hawk he named Frightful.
7. Sam boiled hickory sticks, which—when boiled dry—leave a salty residue.
9. Sam made a fireplace in his tree from clay and dry grass.
10. Sam cut out more knotholes from the tree to let additional oxygen in since the burning fire had used it all up.

Bonus Box: Answers will vary.

Page 133
Possible answers:
1. There are rumors that the house is haunted. The Darrows have scared away anyone who rented the house.
2. Thomas is bothered and angry about it. Mr. Small is also disturbed. Mrs. Small likes the furniture arrangement. Thomas is distrustful of Mr. Pluto.
3. Thomas decides to investigate the hole under the porch and falls into the hidden passageway. He becomes frightened by a sound in the tunnel, drops his flashlight, and becomes disoriented.
4. Mr. Pluto chases Thomas in the woods. Even though Mr. Pluto is lame in one leg, he's able to run Thomas down and even pick him up.
5. The Small family finds the three triangles. Mr. Small decides that he and Thomas will have to stand watch during the night.
6. Mr. Small goes to confront Mr. Pluto because he thinks Mr. Pluto vandalized their kitchen. While looking for Mr. Pluto, he and Thomas find the secret cavern.
7. Mr. Pluto has become sick and weak. He's worried that the Darrows will take advantage of him and find the treasure now that he's sick.
8. Mayhew hears from Carr that a new family has moved into the house. He decides that he must make sure they leave his father alone and don't discover whatever his father is hiding from the Darrows.
9. They frighten and embarrass the Darrows so much that the Darrows will probably stop bothering Mr. Pluto.
10. Mr. Pluto is able to relax and stop worrying about the treasures. Thomas and Mr. Small will probably spend a lot of time in the cavern inventorying the treasures.